ISBN 978-1-397-36742-6
PIBN 11377403

This book is a reproduction of an important historical work. Forgotten Books uses
state-of-the-art technology to digitally reconstruct the work, preserving the original format
whilst repairing imperfections present in the aged copy. In rare cases, an imperfection in
the original, such as a blemish or missing page, may be replicated in our edition. We do,
however, repair the vast majority of imperfections successfully; any imperfections that
remain are intentionally left to preserve the state of such historical works.

PROCEEDINGS

OF THE

SUPREME COUNCIL

—: OF :—

SOVEREIGNS GRAND INSPECTORS GENERAL OF THE THIRTY-THIRD AND LAST DEGREE

ANCIENT AND ACCEPTED

SCOTTISH RITE

FOR THE

OMINION OF CANADA,

HELD AT THEIR " GRAND EAST, MONTREAL," 45°, 31' N. LAT., AND 73°, 20' W. LONG., MERIDIAN OF GREENWICH,

ON THE

NINTH DAY OF OCTOBER, A. D. 1878.

THOS. DOUGLAS HARINGTON, 33°, OTTAWA,
M∴ P∴ Sov∴ Gr∴ Commander.

JOHN WALTER MURTON, 33°, HAMILTON,
Secretary General H∴ E∴

HAMILTON :
TIMES PRINTING COMPANY, 3 HUGHSON STREET.
1878.

PROCEEDINGS

OF THE

Supreme Council of the 33°

OF THE

ANCIENT AND ACCEPTED SCOTTISH RITE

OF FREEMASONRY,

FOR THE

DOMINION OF CANADA.

——┼· 1878. ·┼——

Pursuant to summons, and in accordance with the Statutes, THE MOST PUISSANT SUPREME COUNCIL OF THE 33RD AND LAST DEGREE OF FREEMASONRY assembled in Annual Session, at the Headquarters of the Rite, in the city of Montreal, on Wednesday, the 9th day of October, V∴ E∴ 1878, corresponding with the 12th day of the Hebrew month *Tisri*, 5639.

The roll being called, the following were found to be present :—

OFFICERS:

Illustrious Brother THOMAS DOUGLAS HARINGTON,
M∴ P∴ Sov∴ Grand Commander.

" ROBERT MARSHALL,
P∴ Lieut∴ Grand Commander.

" JOHN WALTER MURTON,
Secretary General H∴ E∴

" WILLIAM HENRY HUTTON,
Grand Marshal.

" ISAAC HENRY STEARNS,
Grand Standard Bearer.

" WILLIAM REID,
Grand Captain of the Guard.

MEMBERS:

Illustrious Brother COL. W. J. B. MCLEOD MOORE,
Representative of the Sup∴ Councils of England and Wales, and Greece.

' " EUGENE MORTIMER COPELAND,

" HUGH MURRAY,

" BENJAMIN LESTER PETERS,
Deputy for Prince Edward Island.

Those who did not answer to their names were,
Illustrious Brother HUGH ALEXANDER MACKAY,
Hamilton, Treasurer General H∴ E∴

" JOHN VALENTINE ELLIS,
St. John, Grand Chancellor.

" DAVID RANSOM MUNRO,
St. John, Grand Master of Ceremonies.

" ROBERT THOMSON CLINCH,
St. John, Deputy for Nova Scotia.

" HUGH WILLIAMS CHISHOLM, St. John.

" JAMES DOMVILLE, St. John.

" JAMES K. KERR, Toronto.

The Supreme Council was opened in full form at 12.30 o'clock.

Letters explaining the cause of their absence were read from

Ill.·. Bro.·. HUGH A. MACKAY,
"   "   JOHN V. ELLIS,
"   ."   ROBERT T. CLINCH,

which were, on motion, accepted as satisfactory.

Ill.·. Bro.·. PETERS explained the cause of the non-attendance of Ill.·. Bros.·. DOMVILLE, CHISHOLM and MUNRO, stating that he expected the former would be present before the close of the session, and that the two latter, he thought, had written the Secretary General, giving their reasons for not being in their places in the Council. The explanation was accepted by the Council for this session.

Ill.·. Bro.·. GEORGE O. TYLER, 33°, Deputy of the S.·. C.·. N.·. J.·. United States, for the State of Vermont, was announced, admitted and welcomed.

Ill.·. Bro.·. W. H. HUTTON moved, seconded by Ill.·. Bro.·. I. H. STEARNS, that the proceedings of this Council at the session of 1877 having been printed and distributed, their reading be dispensed with, and that the same be now confirmed.—Carried.

The Sov.·. Grand Commander being called from the Throne, it was occupied temporarily by the Lieut.·. Grand Commander.

Letters were read from the following Illustrious Brethren (members of foreign Supreme Councils), in answer to invitations extended to them by the Sec.·. Gen.·. viz :—

Ill.·. Bro.·. J. H. DRUMMOND, Sov.·. Gr.·. Com.·. Sup.·. Co. . N.·. J.·. United States.
"   "   A. G. GOODALL, Active Member   do.
"   "   V. L. HULBURT,   do.   do.
"   "   H. A. JOHNSON,   do.   do.

also from Ill.·. Bro.·. ALBERT PIKE, Sov.·. Gr.·. Com.·. S.·. J.·. United States, sent through Ill.·. Bro.·. COL. MOORE.

The Sovereign Grand Commander resumed the Throne and delivered his annual address as follows :—

ADDRESS

To the Supreme Council 33° Ancient and Accepted Scottish Rite of the Dominion of Canada, and the Officers and Members thereof, GREETING :

ILLUSTRIOUS BRETHREN,—

For the fifth time we are permitted, by Divine Goodness, to assemble together in annual Session, and once more I have the happiness of recording that, during the past year, no vacancy has occurred in our ranks—our companionship remaining intact. I have not much wherewith to detain you from the real work of our Council, for with the exception of one or two matters to which I will presently allude, all has gone on so smoothly that my own honorable office has almost proved a sinecure. I have to offer my thanks to our Illustrious Deputies and energetic Secretary General for this, and to their respective Reports, as well as that of our Illustrious Treasurer General, I refer you for full information, more than I can furnish, both statistically and financially. Speaking generally, I know the Rite is progressing, but I think that this satisfactory state of things would become more marked if our respective Deputies, and indeed if each and every of our active 33rds were empowered by the Council to visit places they might deem large enough to support Lodges of Perfection, and select from among the Craft there good material, and there and then confer the Degrees from the 4° to 16° on the minimum number of members required by our Constitution, to establish a Lodge of Perfection, etc., such parties so received pledging themselves to the work of propagating the A.·. & A.·. S.·. Rite. It is always hard to bring a body of men away from their homes. I merely offer this as a suggestion, leaving the details, should the Council approve the principle, to be worked out by a Committee. I have conversed on this matter with the Ill.·. Secretary General, who is prepared with a scheme for carrying it into effect. I think such a course is adopted by other Supreme Councils.

I have granted *Warrants* for separate Lodges of Perfection, one at *Toronto*, and the other at *St. John*, New Brunswick. I had the pleasure of being present at a meeting at Hamilton of the Ontario Consistory 32°, and witnessing the admirable working of the 30° Kadosh there. I was shown the rooms set apart at Toronto for the working of the Rite, which were appropriate and convenient, and do credit to our Brethren. I would have visited London, but could not accomplish it. I was however assured that our Brethren there were greatly exerting themselves. The Montreal Bodies need no express mention here. We are eye witnesses of their value to the Rite, and any personal praise from me would be superfluous. Respecting our Brethren of the Maritime Provinces, I am unable to tender my personal report, but I am rejoiced to be able to say that their energy and perseverance have, as I understand, conquered the effects of the terrible fire and serious losses incurred in New Brunswick.

Our *Relations* with *Sister Supreme Councils* continue to be all we can desire, although the Exchanges of Representatives have not yet been completely established. I may mention that Representatives are appointed near Ireland, Switzerland, Brazil and Colon, and I have recommended Representatives near us for Switzerland, Brazil, Colon, France and Italy. Spain and Mexico have, during the year, sought our recognition, and their letters will be presented to you. There are other Councils, whose standing has not yet been arrived at, and with which we have no correspondence. Our Illustrious Secretary General will supply particulars.

Some of our Sister Councils have had to mourn the *loss* by *death* during the past year of several invaluable members, and our warmest sympathy for such losses has been conveyed on behalf of our Council to those who have suffered. It is known that the Masonic Fraternity has, in common with their other fellow creatures, been desolated by the very terrible *yellow fever plague* that has been committing such ravages in some of the Southern parts of the United States, doubtless, permitted by God for some good purpose of his own. Of course many of our Brethren, members of the A.˙. & A.˙. Scottish Rite must have succumbed to the common calamity. They are at rest, but to those they have left behind, sympathy and help, where possible, must be acceptable and comforting. You will probably choose to have an embodiment of your sentiments hereon recorded and forwarded.

I offer, in conclusion, some general remarks, for which I trust I shall not be deemed presumptuous. Notice of motion was given last year in relation to the absence of Members of the Supreme Council from our annual sessions, and the declaring their seats vacant as Active Members. You are aware that some Brethren have not hitherto appeared at all—not thinking it worth while even to forward written apologies and excuses. This is neither correct nor courteous, and should not be. The work of the A.˙. and A.˙. Scottish Rite should be shared and carried on by all. It does seem to me that the Rite is looked upon by some, more as a kind of Side Degree than as a distinct and important body, to belong to which ought to be deemed a privilege. It would seem that Brethren, having attained high rank in other branches of Freemasonry, (for which they had, however, to work), consider the right of placing 33° opposite their names as a kind of reward for services foreign to the A.˙. and A.˙. Scottish Rite. This is unfair to their Brother 33rds, who, instead, acknowledge their specific duties to the Rite and strive to fulfil them. Our numbers are necessarily few, and it is of importance, therefore, that every active 33rd should give to our body the benefit of his presence and counsel once a year. The actual meeting and communion together should have a good effect, and conduce to good fellowship, and our Subordinate Bodies cannot fail to appreciate our labours better, when the published proceedings show them, that their Active Chiefs take a palpable and practical interest in their welfare, as well as that of the Rite generally.

I am rather afraid to speak of "Harmony" prevailing everywhere. Differences exist between our Toronto Members, and charges have been preferred in the Ontario Consistory, one against another, for language used of a nature anything but masonic and creditable. I understand that such charges were in course of regular inquiry, and mutual friends were hoping to settle differences by urging mutual forbearance; but I grieve to inform the Council that an appeal has been made to the Civil Courts in a suit for libel, and our Ill.·. Secretary General and others are subject to be dragged forward to give testimony on a masonic affair. This is so opposed, in my opinion, to every principle and attribute of the A.·. and A.·. S.·. Rite, that I feel constrained to introduce the disagreeable subject into my address as a duty, in the hope that the Supreme Council will think proper to express a very decided condemnation thereon, and that the scandal may thus be avoided.

I regret to occupy your time, but I have one more matter to which I invite your attention and consideration. Information was conveyed to me that parties from the United States of America had addressed invitations to members of the A.·. & A.·. S.·. Rite in Canada to establish what are called the respective Rites of "*Mizraim*" and "*Memphis*," and promising easy admittance thereto to parties owing allegiance and obedience to our Supreme Council, who were told that the essentials in all were alike. I lost no time in transmitting to our various Bodies letters of caution and warning, (copy of which will be exhibited by our Illustrious Secretary General,) the issuing of which, I have reason to believe, had a salutary effect. But I am sorry to state that a document (which I hardly know how to give an exact name to,) was subsequently circulated, bearing no signature, but born at Maitland, in Ontario. There appeared likewise an article in a Masonic publication, *The Craftsman*, relating to the above named Rites, and added thereto another styled the "*Ancient and Primitive Rite.*" The first document contained a list or roll of some thirty Bodies, and an offer was made to confer their Degrees at a certain cost—such cost to be, however, less in amount if the entire List or Roll was conferred at once. Nothing, I apprehend, could more surely tend to prostitute and lower Freemasonry than this act, and serve to render it ridiculous in the estimation of the public at large.

The article in the *Craftsman* (which I append,) purported to give a correct list of all the Degrees appertaining to the before named three Rites, with explanations of their several meanings, etc.; but the article did more, it told the members of the A.·. & A.·. Scottish Rite that they would be willingly welcomed, because they possessed already certain secrets which would be shown to be the same as those to be made known as belonging to the before named three Rites— Rites looked upon in general as spurious, and not to be recognized.

There is, in my mind, no doubt but the offer to receive our members was an attempt to cause them to violate *Obligations*, because they could not if received as proposed, appear without divulging what they had solemnly promised not to reveal, except to brethren lawfully entitled to exchange the same with them. The author of both documents perpetrated a decided breach of his own Obligation and his vow of allegiance as a member of the A.·. & A.·. Scottish Rite, and I fear adopted the course he did as an act of defiance I hope I am mistaken

An opinion was published by Ill.·. Bro.·. ALBERT PIKE, 33°, (see Appendix)

as regards the *Rite of Memphis*, and which I apprehend will apply equally to the other named Rites.

I am very sure that brethren who have ceased to be affiliated with our Bodies are just as subject to the laws of the A∴ & A∴ S∴ Rite, and to be disciplined, suspended, or expelled, if proved to merit punishment, as though they were subscribing members. I hope the Supreme Council will not separate without recording a clear verdict in relation to the mischievous Rites, to which I have already alluded, and prohibiting its several Bodies and Members from acknowledging what are simply attempted to be introduced into Canada for the purpose of interfering with the existing harmony and prosperity of our Body. In conclusion, allow me to finish according to Masonic usage by praying that our labours thus begun in order, may be conducted in peace, and closed in harmony. So mote it be !

 T. DOUGLAS HARINGTON, 33°,

Sov∴ Gr∴ Com∴ &c.

Montreal, 9th Oct., 1878.

It was moved by Ill∴ Bro∴ PETERS, seconded by Ill∴ Bro∴ HUTTON, that the address of the M∴ P∴ Sov∴ Gr∴ Com∴ be referred to a special Committee to recommend action thereon.—Carried.

The Sov∴ Gr∴ Commander appointed the following as the committee :—Ill∴ Bros∴ PETERS, HUTTON and MARSHALL.

The Supreme Council was then called from labor.

The Supreme Council resumed labor at 2.30 o'clock.

The following resolution was then moved by Ill∴ Bro∴ HUTTON, seconded by Ill∴ Bro∴ COPELAND, that in view of the fact that Montreal Consistory is now quite unable to work in conformity with the constitution, as there are only two 33rds resident in the city, that Ill∴ Bro∴———be elected to receive the 33rd and last degree of the A∴ & A∴ S∴ Rite, and as the emergency is an exceptional one, that the Secretary General be instructed to take the vote of the absent members of the Sup∴ Co∴ by telegraph, and, if elected, that Ill∴ Bro∴———receive the degree before the closing of the present session of the Sup∴ Council. —Carried.

The Secretary General then despatched telegraphs to the absent members of the Council for their votes on the above subject, and received objections to the election as being in violation of one of the Articles of the Constitution.   All, however, heartily endorsed the Ill.·. Brother.

Communications from the following foreign Supreme Councils, were read, viz :—

> Southern Jurisdiction U. S. A.
> Mexico,
> Colon,
> New Granada,
> San Domingo,
> Peru,
> England,
> Ireland,
> Scotland,
> Belgium,
> Switzerland,
> Spain.

Also an extract from a letter of the Ill.·. Bro.·. His Imperial Highness THE PRINCE RHODOCANAKIS, Sov.·. Gr.·. Com.·. Sup.·. Co.·. of Greece, written to Ill.·. Bro.·. COL. MOORE, representative of that Sup.·. Council, sending his warmest regards and assurances of the sympathy and affection of his Supreme Council towards the Sup.·. Council of Canada.

It was moved by Ill.·. Bro.·. PETERS, seconded by Ill.·. Bro.·. COPELAND, that the preceding letters be referred to the Committee on Foreign Correspondence and Relations.— Carried.

The petitions which had been received from the Brethren of Toronto and St. John for warrants for lodges of Perfection for these cities, separate from the Chapters of Rose Croix, and which warrants had been issued by the M.·. P.·. Sov.·. Gr.·. Com.·. since the last session of this Council, were presented and ordered to be recorded.

The following communication from Toronto Chapter of Rose Croix was read :—

TORONTO CHAPTER ROSE CROIX OF H∴ R∴ D∴ M∴

Resolution passed at the regular Assembly of the above Chapter on the 28th day of November, A. D., 1877.

Moved by Ill∴ Bro∴ F. J. MENET, 32°, seconded by Sov∴ Prince GEO. WATSON, 18°, that, whereas, Sov∴ Prince SAMUEL GEORGE STRONG 18,° a member of this Chapter, has pleaded guilty to the crime of forgery at the last assizes held in Toronto, and has been sentenced to a term of imprisonment in the Provincial Penitentiary, which he is now serving, and has thereby become a felon in the eyes of the law; therefore, this Chapter deems and declares that the said SAMUEL GEORGE STRONG is unworthy to be continued as a member thereof, and hereby suspends him from all privileges, and recommends him for expulsion from the Rite, by the Supreme Council. Carried.

THOS. SARGANT, 32°, M∴ W∴ Sov∴

J. ERSKINE, 18°, Registrar.

On motion of Ill∴ Bro∴ H. MURRAY, seconded by Ill∴ Bro∴ I. H. STEARNS, the resolution and recommendation of Toronto Chapter regarding Bro∴ S. G. STRONG was referred to the Committee on the Doings of Subordinate Bodies.

The M∴ P∴ Sov∴ Gr∴ Commander then called for the Reports of the Provincial Deputies, which were forthcoming only from the Ill∴ Deputies of Quebec and Ontario, and were read as follows :—

PROVINCE OF QUEBEC.

MONTREAL, Oct. 7th, 1878.

To the Supreme Council, 33°, for the Dominion of Canada.

ILLUSTRIOUS BRETHREN :--

As our annual session once more comes round, it becomes again, not only my duty but a great pleasure to make my report as to the condition of our beloved Rite in the Province over which I hold your commission as Special Deputy.

During the past year I am most happy to report that the greatest harmony and good order has uninterruptedly existed between the various bodies and their members.

Owing to the continued and apparently endless depression, which, during the past five years has held sway, and which now shows no signs of a break in the clouds, the additions to our ranks have not been numerous, but the high standard of quality has been effectually maintained, and the work has been well and impressively performed.

The separation of the Lodge of Perfection from the Chapter of Rose Croix seems to work well, and under its present enthusiastic head, will, I feel sure, continne to do so.

I much regret to say that I have not been able to start any new bodies, as under the peculiar state of opinion in this Province, the Rite is practically confined to the City of Montreal.

My endeavours, however, in this direction will not cease, and I trust next year to report some additions.

The whole respectfully submitted.

W. H. HUTTON, 33°,

Deputy, Province of Quebec.

PROVINCE OF ONTARIO.

OFFICE OF THE DEPUTY

FOR THE PROVINCE OF ONTARIO,

HAMILTON, 9th Oct., 1878.

To the Supreme Council, 33°, for the Dominion of Canada.

ILLUSTRIOUS BRETHREN :

I am again called upon in accordance with my duty to give to the Supreme Council a report of the condition and doings of the Rite in the Province of Ontario, and am happy in being able to say that, although no extension of the Rite has taken place to other cities and towns since last year, owing to the continued depression of the times, the old Bodies are all progressing as well as can be expected, and considerable additions have been made to their membership.

I have visited the Bodies in this jurisdiction with the exception of London, and find that very considerable progress has been made in the manner and style of conferring the Degrees.

The Brethren of the Toronto Chapter Rose Croix, in answer to the invitation given them by the Sup.˙. Council, agreed to a separation of the Lodge of Perfection from the Chapter, and formally presented a petition for a Warrant, which the Sov.˙. Gr.˙. Com.˙. granted, and on the 21st May last I proceeded to that city, accompanied by a number of the Ill.˙. members of Moore Consistory, inaugurated and constituted under the Warrant the new Lodge by the name of "Toronto Lodge of Perfection," and installed its Officers, and on the same occasion, by invitation of the M.˙. W.˙. S.˙. installed the newly elected Officers of Toronto Chapter of Rose Croix, and was sumptuously entertained.

I have to report that during the year information came to me from various sources that it was contemplated by some members of our Obedience to establish in the city of Toronto and elsewhere, Bodies called Chapters of Rose Croix 18°, under a system termed the " Ancient and Primitive Rite," and further, there appeared in the *Craftsman* a long descriptive article of this system, comparing it with others, and endeavouring to show the identity of several of its Degrees with those of the Ancient and Accepted Scottish Rite ; and still further, there was inserted in the Toronto *Mail* newspaper of the 21st May, an article stating that the Rite was being or had been established in that city, and invited members of the A.·. & A.·. S.·. Rite to visit Bodies of their system.   When matters had arrived at this state, I communicated the information to the M.·. P.·. Sov.·. Gr.·. Com.·. who issued a circular to all Bodies of our Obedience, warning their members not to take part in this movement, nor have any Masonic intercourse with members of the same in matters touching any of the Degrees of the A.·. & A.·. S.·. Rite, as such intercourse would be in violation of their obligations in this Rite.   This timely action I think has had the effect of reminding those Brethren of their duties, and since that time I have heard nothing of the A.·. & P.·. R.·. in the City of Toronto. However, this Rite is advertised in a sheet issued in the Village of Maitland, which sets forth 30 Bodies conferring 282 Degrees, and I rejoice to know, and I feel sure the members of this Sup.·. Council will be pleased to find, that no Bodies of the A.·. & A.·. S.·. R.·. figure in this list of Degrees by wholesale, a copy of which document was sent to me by some party in Maitland, who placed his initials upon the wrapper, and which I submit with this report.   I now bring the subject before the Sup.·. Council, that the question of dual membership may be fully considered, and a decision arrived at, as to whether a member of the A.·. & A.·. S.·. Rite of our Obedience can be a member also of a System which pretends to confer some of our Degrees and also propagate this System or any other System which confers Degrees of the same name and purporting to be identical with ours.

I am happy to state that the Bodies of this Rite in this Province are constantly visited by members of the Rite from the Northern and Southern Jurisdictions of the U. S., and a continual intercourse of the most fraternal character exists between the members and Bodies of the Rite in this Province.

I had the pleasure and privilege in February last of attending the re-union of the A.·. & A.·. S.·. R.·., which annually takes place in the City of Cincinnati, Ohio, where it is and has been for years worked to perfection in a manner said to be superior to any place on the Globe, and am happy to report that this Sup.·. Co.·. was again (as in previous years it had been on similar occasions), honored in being mentioned in the most hearty manner, and many wishes were expressed for our success and prosperity.   The Ill.·. Bro.·. E. T. CARSON, who so ably presides over Ohio Consistory, I had hoped to have seen with us to-day.

I have only to add in closing this report that the A.·. & A.·. S.·. Rite has firmly established itself in this Province, and I sincerely trust that the good times so long looked forward to will soon come, and the Craft in many places, feeling able to bear the burden, may be induced to undertake the work of a Lodge of Perfection, and that by another year I hope to be able to report that the Bodies of the Rite have been greatly increased in the Province of Ontario.

Respectfully and fraternally submitted,

J. W. MURTON, 33°,

Deputy, Province of Ontario.

Moved by Ill∴ Bro∴ MURRAY, seconded by Ill∴ Bro∴ REID, that the Reports of the Deputies, as read, be received. —Carried.

Ill∴ Bro∴ B. L. PETERS, on behalf of the Chairman, presented the Report of the Committee on Foreign Correspondence and Relations.

To the M∴ P∴ Sovereign Grand Commander and members of the Supreme Council, 33°, of Canada.

The Committee on Foreign Correspondence and Relations submit the following report :

All our relations with the foreign Supreme Councils, with which we are in correspondence, are of the most agreeable character.

THE NORTHERN JURISDICTION, UNITED STATES.

The Supreme Council for the Northern Jurisdiction of the United States held its Session for the present year at Milwaukee, Wisconsin, in September. The attendance of members was large, but the business transacted seems to have been chiefly of a local character.

THE SOUTHERN JURISDICTION, UNITED STATES.

The Supreme Council for the Southern Jurisdiction of the United States, held its biennial session at Washington, in May of the present year. The Committee are indebted to Ill∴ Bro∴ Fred Webber, 33°, Treasurer General, for a copy of the proceedings. In his allocution, the Sov∴ Grand Commander speaks hopefully of the Rite in that jurisdiction. One or two passages of interest are extracted : "It is a true saying of the wise and good Roman Emperor, Marcus Antoninus, (Aurelius) : 'Be aware, therefore, that every man is worthy, just so much as the things are worth about which he busies himself'. If our labour to build up an Ancient and Accepted Scottish Rite had no higher purpose than to make it strong in numbers and prosperous by popularity, thereby to gain importance in our own estimation, or in the opinion of others ; if we had nothing to teach, by which to make men better and wiser ; if we endeavoured only to make our degrees impressive and striking by stage show and scenic effect; if the symbols of Masonry had for us no profound and recondite meaning, the work we do would be but waste of time, little worthy of us, and little worth doing in an age when there is so much real work to do, so much to learn and so little time to devote to study.

"The work is worthy of us, and our time is not miss-spent in doing it, because the Rite has higher purposes, and contains in itself the means for effecting them. Our symbols teach the great truths of religion and philosophy. Our lectures teach and inculcate a grand system of morals. We labour for the enlightenment of the Craftsmen in every country and speaking every tongue. We assist in emancipating men from error, in liberating them from the bondage of tyranny, and the shackles of craft, and the oppressions that enslave consciences and punish freedom of thought and speech by excommunication." Again he says "The Rite grows, not largely, not everywhere, but with a healthy growth, and in many places, in despite of many hindrances and adverse circumstances. By degrees the waste places are becoming fruitful vineyards and cultivated fields." He adds, "The Ancient and Accepted Scottish Rite needs no one to vindicate it against aspersions. It possesses the keys of true interpretation of the Ancient symbols, older by ages than Pythagoras, which represented and expressed the holy doctrine taught him by the Median Magi. Known to us to express this, their symbols have become for us Divine oracles, teaching the profoundest truths, and by their very presence in the Lodge, making it indeed a sanctuary into which it is a sacrilege for those to enter who are unworthy.

"The truths themselves are neither new to us nor exclusively ours. All doctrines that ever were are public now, promulgated and placarded for all the world to read. And though masonry is ennobled by the truths it teaches, and most ennobled when the sphere of its truths is highest ; and though its symbols are infinitely more august, and by proprietorship of them, it is infinitely richer, if they reveal to the adept the profoundest truths of religion and philosophy ; though that masonry is lowest which sees in its symbols trivial and sterile meanings only ; and that highest which sees in them the expression of the profoundest truths in regard to God and nature, yet it is in itself excellent only in proportion as its lessons and its influences strengthen the ties of Brotherhood, cause men to think themselves and others of a higher nature and heirs of a nobler destiny, impart to them thereby a higher nature and nobler principles of action, with more worthy ends and aims to strive for, and make them better and truer, more tolerant, generous and unselfish.

"Merit does not consist in knowledge, or in doctrine, but in action. Our masonry does not consist of symbolism alone; what its chief titles to honor and reverence are, those know who have taken its degrees, and heard and read its teachings, and seen the effects of its influences upon men.

"Some of our Brethren are disheartened and discouraged, because immediately around them the Rite makes no progress, and men loose interest in it, and cease to labour, and the Bodies are inert and languish, or die outright. I look over the whole broad field and backward to the beginning of the year 1866, and am not discouraged. When our civil war ended, we had no working bodies anywhere, outside of Louisiana. On the Pacific coast we had not one subordinate. Our books were written but not printed, and we had no revenue ; many of us, impoverished by the war, and compelled by constant labour to earn our daily bread, had neither time nor money wherewith to render service to the Rite. See how it has grown and spread since then, and what a work we have done, against prejudices, overcoming opposition amid discouragements. Occasional reverses and periods of depression are inevitable in the life of an Order. Zeal will slacken and interest will flag, and men of whom we expected much will disappoint us. Labour and tillage will often seem to be bestowed in vain upon grateful soil : bodies too numerously and hastily made will live an unhealthy life a little while and then die, and the seed sown will sometimes lie long in the ground before it germinates. There will be here and there no sign of life for years, and we feel ourselves growing old and see no good come of our work, until we are ready to cry " Vanity of vanities, all is vanity and vexation of spirit." But by and by some man steps forward or some influence acts unexpectedly, and the Rite stands on its feet again alert and active."

If any member of our Supreme Council is disheartened let him think of Brother Pike's cheerful words and take heart again.

The business transacted at the session was principally of a local character. A new constitution was adopted, which fixes the number of active members at thirty-three.

Bro.·. MATHEW COOKE, 33°, of London, presented to the Supreme Council a magnificent compilation of music, selected and original, and all arranged by himself,for which he declined to receive other compensation than thanks. The money value of this compilation is estimated at thirty-five hundred dollars. ·It is complete for all the degrees and ceremonies. " No man," says the Sovereign Grand Commander, "has ever begun and completed so great a work for any order or association." Ill.·. Bro.·. PIKE makes a proposal to abolish the many high sounding titles which are still retained in this Rite, and in this proposition he is supported by Ill.·. Bro.·. TOWNSEND, of the Supreme Council for Ireland. The Supreme Council had scarcely closed its sitting before the death was announced of the Illustrious Lieutenant Grand Commander, JOHN ROBIN McDANIEL, whose kindly, generous, and truthful nature had endeared him alike to his chief and to his associates.

MEXICO.

We have received several printed communications from the Supreme Council of Mexico, of which Ill.·. Bro.·. ALFRED CHAVERO is Grand Commander, and EUGENIE CHAVERO, Ill.·. Secretary General. They are mostly in connection with the internal affairs of that Supreme Council. There are disputes and troubles in Mexico arising out of the question of the control of the Symbolic degrees ; the Supreme Council claims authority over the three degrees ; the Lodges have set up an authority for themselves ; the Supreme Council has expelled some members of its obedience who are concerned in the new movement. It would be wise for all Supreme Councils to abandon control over the Symbolic degrees. This would promote harmony, whilst it would not interfere with good government. We do not read with any satisfaction notices of the excommunication of Masons, because they have sought to establish " a Masonry of three degrees," the crime for which some Brethren appear to have been expelled in Mexico. Perhaps the influence of our good example and our good advice might have some effect on the Supreme Council of Mexico. There seems to be no reason why we should not enter into fraternal relations with it. The Committee recommend that this be done.

NEW GRENADA.

We receive the printed official organ *Repertorio Masonico* of the Supreme Council of New Grenada, published at Cartagena. The Sovereign Grand Commander is JUAN MANUEL GRAW, and the Supreme Council is recognized as regular by the Supreme Council for the Southern Jurisdiction of the United States. The Committee recommend that this Supreme Council ask it to exchange representatives.

ST. DOMINGO.

Communications have been received from a Supreme Council at Santo Domingo, capital of the Republic of that name. We are not in fraternal correspondence with that Supreme Council, and have not even the means of knowing whether it is a regular body of the Rite to recognize, and are in correspondence with the Supreme Council of Colon, which originally had Jurisdiction over the territory of San Domingo. The latter is now, however, an independent country, and would seem to be entitled to a Supreme Council. Until further and fuller information can be obtained, the Committee recommend that no action be taken.

PERU.

The Supreme Council of Peru, with which we are in fraternal correspondence, has published a statement of reasons which lead it to demand that the next sitting of the Convent of Confederated Councils shall be the last held. The principal reason it assigns for this demand is that the Confederation has not promoted harmony in the Rite. The Supreme Council for Switzerland, the executive power of the Confederation has issued a reply to the Peruvian circular in which it denies the general correctness of the statements contained in that circular. It says that it fears some occult influences are at work in several bodies of the Rite against the Confederation, for it observes the same symptoms in the Supreme Councils of Peru, of Canada, and of Italy. We might remind our Swiss Brethren that this Supreme Council never entered the Lausanne Confederation, and for the reason that it did not commend itself to our judgment as likely to prove beneficial to the Rite. Time has fully demonstrated the correctness of our view.

It may be noted as of some interest that the Supreme Council of Peru permits the Lodges of its obedience to fraternize with the Symbolic Lodges existing in Peru, holding of the Grand Lodge of Scotland and governed by a Provincial Grand Lodge at Lima.

BRAZIL.

We have nothing of special importance from the Supreme Council of Brazil. The Committee, however, regret to observe that that Supreme Council on the 17th October, lost by death one of its most active members, viz:—Ill.·.Bro.·.Udo Schleusner, a brother profoundly versed in the laws of our Institution, one of the first in the performance of masonic duty, and one of the most vigorous defenders of Masonic unity in Brazil.

ENGLAND.

We have received from the Supreme Council of England a communication announcing the cessation of intercourse with the Grand Orient of France because of its new declaration of principles.

Under this heading, the Committee are constrained to call attention to the cessation of friendly relations between the Supreme Councils for England and Scotland. The divergence of feeling began with the Lausanne Confederation, and it has continued over the question of the Jurisdictional rights of each Supreme Council in the colonies and the territories of the empire. This question is one in which the Supreme Council of Canada cannot desire to enter. Towards both Supreme Councils it is influenced by the warmest and kindliest feelings. Upon the roll of each it recognizes the names of Masons eminent for the practice of public and private virtues. It derives its original membership through both, and it views with sorrow the proclamations which seek to throw doubts upon the legitimacy of either. The main point at issue unquestionably is the question of Jurisdiction, that is as to whether the Supreme Council for England and Wales has exclusive right, as it contends, to all British Territory outside of Great Britain and Ireland, or whether, as is contended by Scotland, there is a common right in the Supreme Councils of England, Scotland and Ireland. Whilst this Council must continue to deplore this unfortunate dispute, it must for the present, at least, scrupulously refrain from entering into it.

SCOTLAND.

The Annual Reporter of the Supreme Council for Scotland furnishes some details of the " Proceedings at the First Congress of the United Supreme Councils " of the Ancient and Accepted Scottish Rite of Freemasonry, held at Edinburgh, " in September, 1877." But no information is furnished as to what Supreme Councils were represented. It is said, however, that the Supreme Council for the Southern Jurisdiction of the United States, that for Ireland, that for Scotland, for Central America, and for Greece, make up the League, but practi-cally nothing was done, for the Report says :—" The Congress resolved to delay consideration of suggestions for amendments on the Constitutions of the Order and upon the Rituals of the Degrees, until the declaration of Principles and Sec-ondary Articles were considered, and, with or without amendments, adopted by the Councils forming the League." The "declaration of principles" is certainly more agreeable to the feelings and consonant with the views of the members of the Rite in Canada. The first two Articles are :—" Freemasonry proclaims as its necessary and fundamental principle a belief in the existence of a true and living God. 2nd.—It requires from its members an acknowledgment of such belief, leaving to each to worship God in the manner and form which in his own conscience he believes to be most acceptable to Him." Whilst expressing their satisfaction at this declaration, the Committee think that there is no reason whatever why the Supreme Council should retire from its position of last year as respects Leagues or Confederations of Supreme Councils.

Some changes have taken place in the membership of the Supreme Council, owing to the retirement from active labors of Ill.·. Bro.·. THOS. ELDER MAC-RITCHIE and Ill.·. Bro.·. ANDREW KERR, who have been placed on the Honorary roll. There are now eight active members in the Supreme Council, over which Ill.·. Bro.·. J. WHYTE MELVILLE still presides. He is the only one left of the original members of the formation in 1846. The other members are the EARL OF ROSSLYN, LINDSAY MACKERSY, WILLIAM MANN, COL. A. CAMPBELL CAMPBELL, HENRY INGLIS, SIR MICHAEL R. SHAW STEWART and the EARL OF MAR and KELLIE. The names of five Illustrious Brethren appear upon the Honorary roll, and the Supreme Council has also a third-class of Sovereign Grand Inspectors General, one of whom is in China, three are in India, and two in New Zealand.

FRANCE.

So far as your Committee are aware the Supreme Council has never opened fraternal correspondence with the Grand Orient of France. It is not likely to do so now that it has declared a belief in the existence of the Great Architect of the Universe not necessary to admission into the Fraternity. There is no need for this Supreme Council to further express its views upon this matter. We are at one with the Supreme Councils of England and Ireland, and their circulars upon the subject might be printed with our Proceedings of the present year.

BELGIUM.

The Illustrious Secretary General has sent to the Committee an interesting letter received by him as Representative of the Supreme Council of Belgium, from Ill.·. Bro.·. CLUYDTS, our Representative at that Supreme Council. Bro.·. CLUYDTS expresses satisfaction at the plan suggested by this Supreme Council for an interchange of opinions and information through the Representatives. He states some interesting facts respecting the internal workings of the Rite in Belgium. He sends also the Bulletin of the Proceedings of 1876-7, which is published annually in November, and promises to send us the number for each year in the future. There is a great deal that is of much interest in the Proceedings, and the Supreme Council seems to aid many undertakings. It assists the works of education, helps by money a Brother to return to his friends in Central America, aids in opening up Africa, and takes cognizance of the spread of works of all kinds for the benefit of humanity. A *resume* of the proceedings of Foreign Supreme Councils is given, that of Canada included. The

Supreme Council of Belgium is composed of thirty members. The Supreme Council itself appears to confer the Degrees between the 18° and 33°. At page 43, sitting 26th March, 1877, the following curious announcement is made: " The President communicated the Annual Word which is to be transmitted to all the Bodies recognizing the authority of the Supreme Council." The Grand Orator appears to fill an important place, as a Judge in the deliberations of the Supreme Council, and as a Lecturer in instructing newly initiated members.

SWITZERLAND.

Some changes have taken place in the organization and membership of the Supreme Council for Switzerland. The Illustrious Bro.·. JULES BESANÇON, who for a number of years governed that Supreme Council with ability and devotion to its interests, lately declined longer to fill the position. He was succeeded by Ill.·. Bro.·. AMBERNY who had long been Lieutenant Grand Commander. This change took place in April last. It was followed in July by the death of JULES DUCHESNE, the Illustrious Secretary, who, though only thirty-nine years of age, had been one of the most active masons of the Rite in Europe, and whose reputation spread throughout the entire fraternity as the Secretary of the Convent General in 1875. The Supreme Council of Switzerland is composed of nine active members. A short time before the death of Brother DUCHESNE, it announced to us the death of the Illustrious Brother PACHOUD, a distinguished mason, and the representative near that Supreme Council of the Supreme Council of England. Our deepest sympathies go out to our Swiss Brethren in their losses, and we assure them of our sorrow and fraternal affection as the only consolation we have to offer them in their bereavements.

SPAIN.

A communication has been received from a body calling itself a Supreme Council of the Ancient and Accepted Rite, and claiming to have been established in 1811, with its See at Madrid. The Committee have not the means at their command up to the present moment, of ascertaining definitely the regularity of this Supreme Council, which they do not think is recognized by either the Supreme Councils for England or Ireland or Scotland, or by that of the Northern or Southern Jurisdictions of the United States. They do not find in the list of Supreme Councils, published in our Proceedings of 1875, (as those to whose attention the Supreme Council of Canada was commended by Illustrious Brother PIKE,) any mention of the Supreme Council for Spain. It is true that there is a conflict of Masonic Jurisdiction in Spain. It is possible that the Supreme Council of Colon may have regularized the body at Madrid, but the information before the Committee is not sufficient to enable them to give the Supreme Council of Canada opportunity to pronounce intelligently on the subject.

EGYPT.

In the Committee's report last year reference was made to the establishment of a Supreme Council at New Zealand by the Grand Orient of Egypt, whose right to establish a Supreme Council, the Committee said was by no means clear.

It appears that several of the Supreme Councils have had considerable correspondence in regard to this body in Egypt, the result of which has been that the Supreme Council of Egypt has been made a legitimate power of the Rite through the intervention of the Supreme Council for Italy. ·The Committee understand that there is now an application for recognition by the Supreme Council of Egypt before this Supreme Council. In this connection it may be of interest to quote from Bro.·. PIKE's address at the last meeting of his Supreme Council :—" I advise you to acknowledge as a legitimate Power of the Ancient and Accepted Scottish Rite, the Supreme Council of Egypt, as reorganized by a member duly commissioned of the Supreme Council of Italy, and decline to take unfriendly action against the British Councils by entering into relations of amity and mutual representation with the offending power, until it withdraws its support of the so-called Supreme Council of New Zealand. I hope it will see the wisdom of doing this, because it must not expect to be exempt from invasions of its jurisdictions by other Powers if it persists in maintaining a body claiming to be a Supreme Council within the jurisdiction of one or all of the British Councils, because that body never can be recognized by the Supreme Councils of the world, and because the Grand Constitutions forbid the exercise of any power by one Supreme Council within the lawful jurisdiction of another ; and a Supreme Council which sets this fundamental law at nought forfeits its rights to the respect of others, and as a breaker of the law may and should be pronounced by all a common disturber of the peace and an Ishmaelite among the Powers of Scottish Freemasonry. It is time that all these Powers should resolve to enforce the law, that all should defend the violated rights of each, and make the cause of one the cause of all." The Supreme Council adopted the following resolution : *Resolved*— " That the Grand Orient of Egypt (as reorganized under proper Masonic authority), be and is hereby acknowledged as a legitimate and lawful authority. But this Supreme Council declines to enter into amicable relations therewith until its position relative to the establishment of a Supreme Council within the British Possessions be more satisfactorily explained."

The Committee also submit the following extract of a letter from Ill.·. Bro.·. J. WHYTE MELVILLE, 33°, Sovereign Grand Commander of the Supreme Council of Scotland, to Ill.·. Bro.·. PIKE, upon which Bro.·. PIKE and his Supreme Council appear to have acted. The letter is dated 29th April, 1878 :—

" Should you be satisfied that all defects in the Constitution of the Supreme Council of Egypt are now cured, much difficulty in the way of recognition would be removed ; but it appears to me that recognition should be made conditional, on that Council undoing certain acts it has done, and pledging itself in the future to abstain from similar practice. In the first place it has conferred the 33° upon a number of Scotch masons, resident in Scotland, not one of whom ever saw Egypt ; two of these were members of our 30°, and the names of both have since been erased from our roll. No sanction from this Council was asked, nor were we informed of the step which had been taken except through a printed journal. Again it granted the Charter to New Zealand, to which you refer, creating a Supreme Council in British Territory. The case of Canada will no doubt be referred to as justifying the last proceeding, but a moment's reflection will show that the cases are not parallel: 1st, Canada was erected into a Dominion by the British Parliament; 2nd, it had an independent and recognized Grand Lodge and Grand Chapter, and 3rd, the Supreme Council of England, with the consent of this Council and that of Ireland, granted the Charter. This is quite different from New Zealand, which is not erected into a Dominion, has no independent Grand Lodge or Chapter, and the Charter has been granted by an unrecognized and foreign body, in defiance of the protests of the British Councils. If the Supreme Council of Egypt now cancelled the New Zealand Charter and the Diplomas as Sovereign Grand Inspectors General granted to Scotch Brethren *in absence* and agreed to avoid such actings in the future, and you should be satisfied that otherwise it is now healed, I would be disposed to recommend my Council to accede to its recognition."

It might be pointed out that whatever was done by the Supreme Council of Egypt before it became a regular power of the Rite was not lawfully done, and can have no effect. The committee do not feel disposed to recommend the Supreme Council to recognize a body as regular, with which they do not consider it advisable to open fraternal correspondence. They think that in this matter something is due to the feelings of the Supreme Councils of the mother Country, and while that would not influence them to declare a regular body irregular, it at least justifies the recommendation that nothing should be done with undue haste. They recommend that the Grand Chancellor be directed to communicate with the Supreme Councils of England, Scotland and Ireland, sometime before the next meeting of this Supreme Council, and ascertain their views upon this subject.

THE LAUSANNE CONFEDERATION.

The Confederation was to have assembled the present year in London; but we learn from a circular issued on 20th May last that political events had determined the Supreme Council for England to propose the postponement of the meeting for twelve months; and, concurring in the view of the English Council, the Supreme Council for Switzerland, the Executive Power of the Rite, postponed the meeting, and will in due time issue a call for another meeting in which the time and place of holding it will be announced.

A QUESTION OF LAW.

The Supreme Council for the Southern Jurisdiction of the United States submits for the consideration of Sister Supreme Councils, the following to be adopted as a settled principle of the law of the Ancient and Accepted Scottish Rite.

" That in a Dependency, Province or Colony of a country in which there is a " lawful Supreme Council, no foreign power can authorize the creation of a " Supreme Council; and a body so created as a Supreme Council has no legal " existence."

The Committee are quite favorable to the adoption of this principle, as necessary, and recommend it to the favorable consideration of the Supreme Council. They, however, regret that any necessity should exist to limit in any way the Sovereign Powers of Supreme Councils.

The Committee recommend that a memorial page be printed with the report of the proceedings of the present year, containing the names of Ill.·. Brothers John Robin McDaniel, of Virginia, U. S., Lieutenant Grand Commander of the Supreme Council for the Southern Jurisdiction of the United States ; of Odo Schleusner, active member of the Supreme Council of Brazil ; of Orrin Welch, active member of the Supreme Council for the Northern Jurisdiction of the United States ; of ——— Pachoud, active member of the Supreme Council of Switzerland, and of Jules Duchesne, Ill.·. Secretary General of the same Supreme Council, as those of Brothers whose zeal and devotion to the interest of the Rite make their memory worthy of respect and honor.

The Committee also recommend the adoption of the following resolutions :—

1.—That the Sovereign Grand Commander, during the recess of the Supreme Council, take the necessary steps for an exchange of representatives between the Supreme Council of Canada and the Supreme Councils of Mexico and New Grenada.

2.—That the Sovereign Grand Commander cause correspondence to be had with the Supreme Councils for England, Scotland and Ireland in order to ascertain their views as to the legality and standing of the Supreme Council for Egypt as reorganized by the Supreme Council for Italy.

Fraternally submitted,

JOHN V. ELLIS, 33°,
Chairman.

Moved by Ill.·. Bro.·. PETERS, seconded by Ill.·. Bro.·. MOORE, that the Report of the Committee on Foreign Correspondence and Relations be received and laid upon the table.—Carried.

The Report of the Grand Chancellor was then read, as follows :—

OFFICE OF THE GRAND CHANCELLOR,

St. John, N. B., Oct. 1, 1878.

To the M·. P·. Sov. Grand Commander of the Supreme Council, 33°, Ancient and Accepted Scottish Rite for Canada.

Ill.·. Sir and Brother :

I have to report the performance of few official acts as Grand Chancellor.

The Grand Chancellor of the Supreme Council for England and Wales and the Dependencies of the British Crown, in answer to my Circular letter requesting information as to the names of members of the Rite in that Jurisdiction suspended or expelled, in a letter herewith submitted promises the information. Few of the Supreme Councils have directly answered that Circular letter, though I see by the Proceedings of some of them that steps have been taken to comply with our wishes. I believe it will be found that the general conduct of the members of the Rite is so good that few are ever disciplined, and that the correspondence on this subject will always be very light.

I have endeavoured to open up communication with the Representatives of this Supreme Council appointed at the last Session, and have transmitted the Diplomas sent me by the Illustrious Secretary General, issued to Bro.·. HEDGES EYRE CHATTERTON, of Dublin, Ireland ; Bro.·. F. W. RAMSDEN, of St. Jago de Cuba, Representative of Colon ; Bro.·. L. A. D'A. MACEDO, Representative at Brazil, and Bro.·. F. RAMUZ, Representative at Switzerland ; and I hope soon to be in direct correspondence with these Illustrious Brethren.

Previous to the meeting of the Supreme Council for the Northern Jurisdiction of the United States, which lately held its Sitting at Milwaukee, I addressed its Illustrious Secretary General, in the name of this Supreme Council, a Letter of Condolence, on the death of Illustrious Brother ORRIN WELCH, an active Member of that Supreme Council, and Deputy for the State of New York.

As most of the Foreign Affairs of the Supreme Council are treated by the Committee on Foreign Relations, I have the honor to refer the Supreme Council to the Report of that Committee.

Respectfully and fraternally submitted,

JOHN V. ELLIS, 33°,

Grand Chancellor.

On motion of Ill.·. Bro.·. PETERS, seconded by Ill.·. Bro.·. MURRAY, the Report was received.

The Special Committee on Ritual presented their Report, as follows :—

MONTREAL, October 9th, 1878.

To the Supreme Council, 33°, for the Dominion of Canada.

ILLUSTRIOUS BRETHREN :

The Special Council on Ritual are prepared to submit the work revised as far as the 31° and 32°. These being of a judicial and executive character, the Ritual admits of but little dramatic display, and they will be appreciated only by men possessed of intelligent and reflective minds, being literary productions of rare merit.

It is proposed to exemplify the 31° before the Council to-morrow evening, at an hour to be named, and the 32° being exceedingly lengthy and of the character of a summing up or a recapitulation of the teachings of all the degrees, will need in order to be appreciated or judged of, a very careful and attentive hearing, while the same is exemplified to the Sup∴ Co∴   Should the Council elect to have this done, your Committee will take pleasure in doing it whenever it may be deemed advisable.   However the Committee have only to say that the work submitted is that of the S∴ C∴ Southern Jurisdiction, U. S., and sufficiently abbreviated so as to allow of it being conferred, as the length of the work otherwise is so great as to almost preclude the conferring it in one evening.

This is the sum of the labours of your Committee this year, and they plead that the Council will not hold them to a strict account as to their promises made last year, but will indulge them with another term, so as to provide the cere-monials for Inaugurating Bodies, Installation of Officers, etc., which they had hoped to have presented with this report.

Respectfully and fraternally submitted.

J. W. MURTON, 33°,   }
                               } Committee.
WM. H. HUTTON, 33°, }

On motion of Ill∴ Bro∴ PETERS, seconded by Ill∴ Bro∴ MOORE, the Report was received and laid upon the table.

The Council then named half-past eight o'clock as the hour for the exemplification of the 32°.

The following Reports of the Secretary and Treasurer General were read.

REPORT OF THE SECRETARY GENERAL.

OFFICE OF THE SECRETARY GENERAL,

HAMILTON, OCT. 9th, 1878.

To the Supreme Council, 33°, for the Dominion of Canada.

ILL∴ BRETHREN :

I have the pleasure to submit below a statement of the receipts of the Council for the year just ending, as follows :

From Murton Lodge of Perfection,	Hamilton,	- - -		$69 25
" Hochelaga "	"	Montreal,	- - - -	23 .00
" Toronto "	"	Toronto,	- - -	21 75
" Hamilton Chapter Rose Croix,	Hamilton,	- - - -		82 00
" London "	"	London,	- - -	66 75
" Toronto "	"	Toronto, 1877-78	- -	159 50
" Hochelaga "	"	Montreal,	- - -	33 75
" Harington "	"	St. John,	- - - -	26 25

Carried foward,   -   -   - $482 25

	Brought forward,		-	-	-	-	$482	25
From Keith Chapter Rose Croix,	Halifax,	-	-	-			18	50
" Moore Sov∴ Consistory, 32°,	Hamilton.	-	-	-	-		96	00
" Montreal " "	Montreal,	-	-	-	-		110	50
" New Brunswick " "	St. John,	-	-	-	-		9	50
" Proceedings,	-	-	-	-	-	-	1	25

Total,   -   -   · $718 00

All of which has been paid over to the Illustrious Treasurer General.

Respectfully and fraternally submitted.

JOHN W. MURTON, 33°,

Audited and found correct.   *Secretary General.*

WM. REID, 33°.

REPORT OF THE TREASURER GENERAL.

Supreme Council, 33°, for the Dominion of Canada in Account with the Treasurer General.

RECEIPTS.

Oct. 10, 1877, Cash on hand,	-	-	-	-	-	-	$ 777	57
" 8, 1878, " received from Secretary General,			-		-		718	00
Interest to date,	-	-	-	-	-	-	16	59

$1,512 16

EXPENDITURES.

Nov. 5, 1877, Secretary General, Grant for '74, '75 and '76,	-	$200	00
Dec. 21, " *Times* Printing Company, Circulars, July, '77,	-	1	50
" " " Eastwood & Co., Stationery,	- - - -	6	90
" " " J. B. Nixon, Engrossing, -	- - - -	9	70
March 28, 1878, *Spectator* Company, Printing 500 Proceedings, '77,		88	20
" " " Eastwood & Co., Stationery,	- - - -	1	10
Ellis & Armstrong, Printing,	- - - -	3	50
Oct. 5, " Secretary General, Postages, &c.,	- -	18	85
Do. Grant for 1877,	- - -	200	00
W. Bruce, Engraving Certificates and Warrants for '77		37	55
" 8, " Cash Balance on hand,	- - - - -	944	86

$1,512 16

H. A MACKAY, 33°,
     Treasurer General.   Audited and found correct.

WM. REID, 33°,
On behalf of the Committee of Audit and Finance.

Hamilton, Ont., 8th October, 1878.

On motion of Ill∴ Bro∴ MURRAY, seconded by Ill∴ Bro∴ MURTON, these Reports were received and referred to the Committee on Audit and Finance.

The Committee on the Sov∴ Gr∴ Commander's address made a partial report, as follows :—

MONTREAL, 9th Oct., 1878.

To the Supreme Council, 33°, of the Dominion of Canada.

Your Committee on the M∴ P∴ Sov∴ Grand Commander's address recommend that so much of the address as relates to the extension of the powers of Deputies be referred to Ill∴ Bros∴ MURTON, COPELAND and REID.

That so much as relates to the existing difficulties in Ontario be referred to Ill∴ Bros∴ HUTTON, MURRAY and MARSHALL.

That so much as relates to the introduction within this Jurisdiction of Rites known as Memphis, Mizraim, &c., be referred to Ill∴ Bros∴ HUTTON, STEARNS and MURTON.

Your Committee ask leave to make further report.

Respectfully submitted,

B. LESTER PETERS, 33°.
W. H. HUTTON, 33°.
ROBERT MARSHALL, 33°.

It was moved by Ill∴ Bro∴ PETERS, seconded by Ill∴ Bro∴ HUTTON, that the Report be received and adopted. —Carried.

The notice of motion made by Ill∴ Bro∴ H. A. MACKAY, at the last session, was then, on his behalf, taken up, when it was moved by Ill∴ Bro∴ MURTON, seconded by Ill∴ Bro∴ MARSHALL, and resolved

That Article 21, paragraph 1, of the Statutes and Regulations be altered as follows: That the words "betweeen 14° and 16° one month and 16° and 18° one month," be expunged, and the following substituted: "between 14° and 18° two months."

The notice of motion made by Ill∴ Bro∴ ELLIS, at the session of 1877, was also taken up, and on motion of Ill∴ Bro∴ PETERS, seconded by Ill∴ Bro∴ MURRAY, the following was adopted :—

That article 10 of Constitution have the following addition: "But an officer or member whose absence shall extend to three consecutive annual sessions shall, by such absence forfeit his seat and membership, and it shall be the duty of the Sovereign Grand Commander, just before the close of the third session from which such officer or member shall be absent, to pronounce the seat vacant, unless the Supreme Council may see fit to suspend the declaration."

The Supreme Council was then called from labor at eight o'clock and resumed labor again at nine o'clock.

The 32°, or that of "Sublime Prince of the Royal Secret," was then exemplified by the Committee on Ritual, and on motion of Ill.·. Bro.·. PETERS, seconded by Ill.·. Bro.·. REID, the same was adopted as the work to be followed by all Consistories under this Supreme Council.

The Secretary General read a telegram from Ill.·. Bro.·. J. K. KERR, explaining the cause of his absence from this session.

The Supreme Council was called from labor at 10 P. M.

THURSDAY, 10th October.

The Supreme Council resumed its sitting at eleven o'clock A. M.

Ill.·. Bro.·. D. B. TRACY, Representative near the Supreme Council of the Northern Jurisdiction of the United States, was admitted and welcomed.

The Report of the Committee on the Doings of Subordinate Bodies was read, and was as follows :—

To the M.·. P.·. S.·. Gr.·. Commander and Illustrious Brethren of the Supreme Council, 33°, of the A.·. & A.·. S.·. Rite for the Dominion of Canada.

Your Committee on the doings of Subordinate Bodies beg to report as follows :

PROVINCE OF NEW BRUNSWICK.

ST. JOHN.

NEW BRUNSWICK CONSISTORY has done no work during the past year. Membership, 38 ; fees to Supreme Council, $9.50.

HARINGTON CHAPTER OF ROSE CROIX has done no work during the past year. Membership, 65 ; fees to Supreme Council, $16.25.

Your Committee are informed that the Chapter has surrendered its control over the Lodge of Perfection, and for which a separate warrant has recently been issued.

PROVINCE OF NOVA SCOTIA.

HALIFAX.

KEITH CHAPTER OF ROSE CROIX, covering Lodge of Perfection, conferred the 12° on one Brother. Membership, 19 ; fees to Supreme Council, $11.75.

PROVINCE OF ONTARIO.

HAMILTON.

MOORE SOVEREIGN . CONSISTORY conferred the 30° on eight, 31° on thirteen and the 32° on one Brother. Membership, 64 ; fees to Supreme Council, $96.

HAMILTON CHAPTER OF ROSE CROIX conferred the 16° on nine and 18° on five Brethren. Membership, 76 ; fees to Supreme Council, $82.

MURTON LODGE OF PERFECTION conferred the 14° on twelve Brethren, Members withdrawn, two; membership, 94 ; fees to Supreme Council, $66.

LONDON.

LONDON CHAPTER OF ROSE CROIX, covering Lodge of Perfection, conferred the 14° on five, the 16° on four and the 18° on four Brethren. Member restored, 1 ; membership, 43; fees to Supreme Council, $66.75.

TORONTO.

TORONTO CHAPTER OF ROSE CROIX covering for a portion of the year Lodge of Perfection, conferred the 14° on two and the 18° on one Brother. Suspended one, viz : SAMUEL GEORGE STRONG, who affiliated from the Bath Chapter in England. Membership, 51 ; fees to Supreme Council, $28.75.

TORONTO LODGE OF PERFECTION for a portion of the year was held under the warrant of the Toronto Chapter of Rose Croix. Under their own warrant, they have conferred the 4° and 5° on two Brethren. Membership, 63 ; fees to Supreme Council, $21.75.

PROVINCE OF QUEBEC.

MONTREAL.

MONTREAL SOVEREIGN CONSISTORY conferred the 30° on five, the 31° on six and the 32° on nine Brethren. Membership, 42 ; fees to Supreme Council, $110.50.

HOCHELAGA CHAPTER OF ROSE CROIX conferred the 16° on three and the 18° on three Brethren. Members withdrawn, 4 ; membership, 48 ; fees to Supreme Council, $33.75.

HOCHELAGA LODGE OF PERFECTION conferred the 14° on two Brethren. Members withdrawn, 2; membership, 54; fees to Supreme Council, $23.

Respectfully and fraternally submitted,

H. A. MACKAY, 33°,

HAMILTON, Ontario, 7th Oct., 1878.   *Chairman.*

Moved by Ill∴ Bro∴ HUTTON, seconded by Ill∴ Bro∴ REID, that the foregoing Report be received and adopted.— Carried.

The Committee on the Sov∴ Gr∴ Commander's Address made the following final report :—

MONTREAL, 10th Oct., 1878.

To the Supreme Council, 33°, of Canada.

The Committee on the Address of the M∴ P∴ Sov∴ Grand Commander further report :

Your Committee find that the relations of this Supreme Council with Sister Councils, referred to in the Address of the M∴ P∴ Sov∴ Grand Commander, have been fully reported upon by the Committee on Foreign Correspondence, with recommendations in some important cases ; and as the several questions submitted will come before this Council in the consideration of that report, your Committee refrain from any special recommendations on this subject.

Your Committee are in entire accord with the remarks of the M∴ P∴ Sov∴ Grand Commander in the reference made by him to the continued absence from the Annual Session of some members of this Supreme Council. Your Committee hope that the action taken by this Council at the session yesterday upon the notice of motion given last year by the Ill∴ Grand Chancellor will have the effect of securing a better attendance for the future ; but should the default continue your Committee cannot too strongly urge upon the Council the duty of vacating seats as now provided for in the amendment made to the Constitution.

Your Committee are in cordial sympathy with the reference made by the M∴ P∴ Sov∴ Grand Commander to the illustrious dead, called to rest during the past year from sister Jurisdictions, and join in the recommendation made by the "Committee on Foreign Correspondence and Relations," that a Memorial page, recording our deep sense of the loss sustained by the Ancient and Accepted Rite be inscribed in the Proceedings of this Supreme Council.

With special reference to our suffering Brethren in the fever-stricken Cities of the Southern States of America, your Committee recognize the cordial feeling of deep sympathy and commiseration with which the whole Masonic world gives expression to universal sorrow at the terrible affliction with which it has pleased our Heavenly Father to visit those Cities. The great calamity has awakened in their behalf generous aid from every civilized land, to alleviate as far as possible immediate distress. Already from this Dominion the help that it has been in our power to contribute has been heartily rendered, and should the distress increase, and further aid be needed your Committee feel assured that renewed effort will be made to alleviate the distresses of our afflicted Brethren.

Respectfully submitted.

B. LESTER PETERS, 33°
Chairman.
W. H. HUTTON, 33°
ROBERT MARSHALL, 33°

On motion of Ill∴ Bro∴ PETERS, seconded by Ill∴ Bro∴ MURTON, the Report was received and adopted.

The Reports of the several Committees, appointed to consider the statements and suggestions contained in the Address of the Sov∴ Gr∴ Commander, were presented, and were as follows :—

1st. That on the introduction of the Rites of " Memphis," " Mizraim," etc. :—

To the M∴ P∴ Sov∴ Gr∴ Commander and members of the Supreme Council, 33°, for the Dominion of Canada.

Your Committee to whom was referred that portion of the Sov∴ Gr∴ Commander's address which had reference to the introduction of the Rites of Memphis, Mizraim, and the Ancient and Primitive Rite within the Jurisdiction of this Sup∴ Council, beg respectfully to report.

That they consider the establishment of these so-called systems of Masonry as a direct *menace* to the A∴ & A∴ S∴ Rite.

That this act committed by, or attempted to be committed by, members of our obedience is a palpable violation of their fealty of allegiance to this Supreme Council, as these systems pretend to confer many of the degrees of this Rite, and consequently are *rival* in their nature.

That the taking of the degrees of these systems, which are said to be identical with some of the degrees of this Rite, is in direct violation of particular obligations solemnly entered into by members of the A∴ & A∴ S∴ Rite, and consequently deserves the most severe censure ; and a persistent attachment to these other Rites, and more particularly an earnest endeavour to propagate and spread them by members of our obedience (after being made aware of their error in so doing), demands at the hands of this Council the most decided action, and the penalty for such cases provided.

That the articles which have appeared in the *Craftsman* and in other public papers supposed to have been inserted by members of this Rite (who are acting in direct violation of their most solemn obligations) are calculated to have a pernicious effect by enticing brethren, who are uninformed as to the nature of the various systems and who may seek admission, in the belief that they are receiving some of the beautiful degrees of this Rite, and the authors of which should, if discovered, be punished by deprivation of the rights and privileges of the A ∴ & A∴ S∴ Rite.

That the issuing of the advertising sheet or list of degrees in the village of Maitland, referred to in the address of the Sov.∴ Gr.∴ Com.∴, is an act which should stamp the author as a trafficker in degrees, and if a member of the Ancient and Accepted Scottish Rite should subject him to suspension or expulsion ; and your Committee strongly recommend that the Deputy for Ontario be instructed to investigate into the authorship of the Maitland circular, the article in the *Craftsman* and other articles in the public newspapers to which the M.∴ P.∴ Sov.∴ Gr.∴ Commander has referred, and to cause the party or parties, if members of our obedience, to be brought to trial for a violation of their obligations, and if found guilty be punished as the same deserves.

WM. H. HUTTON, 33°,
Chairman.

On motion of Ill.∴ Br.∴ HUTTON, seconded by Ill.∴ Bro.∴ MOORE, the Report was received and adopted.

2d. That on the existing difficulties in Ontario :—

To the Supreme Council, 33°, A∴ & A∴ S∴ Rite for Canada.

ILL.∴ BRETHREN :

The Committee to whom was referred that portion of the Sov.∴ Gr.∴ Commander's address which refers to existing difficulties in Ontario, beg respectfully to submit the following :

They learn with regret that differences exist among the brethren of our obedience in the City of Toronto, Province of Ontario, of a most discreditable nature. Your Committee are surprised to learn that while charges of unmasonic conduct were in regular course of investigation, the matter in dispute was carried into the Civil Courts, and that as a result, officers and members of this Rite may be dragged forward to give testimony in Court on matters Masonic. Your Committee believes that the Rite contains in itself ample means to reach all Brethren charged with Masonic offences, and heartily concur with the Sov.∴ Gr.∴ Commander in stating that such appeal to the Civil Courts is contrary to every principle and attribute of the A∴ & A∴ S∴ Rite, and desire in a most emphatic manner to express their condemnation of such action, and recommend that the Secretary General be instructed to advise the Brother who has taken such action to refrain from pressing his suit, as this Supreme Body, believing that ample means for the redress of Masonic offences is furnished by the Rite, cannot but condemn such action as that indicated.   The Committee trust that harmony will speedily be restored, and that Brethren will constantly remember their obligations, and practice the duty of forgiveness and forgetfulness of injuries inflicted, to the end that peace and concord may prevail, and that the outside world may be enabled truthfully to say : Behold how these Brethren love one another.

W. H. HUTTON, 33°,

Chairman.

On motion of Ill.·. Bro.·. HUTTON, seconded by Ill.·. Bro.·. REID, the Report was received and adopted.

3d. That on the extension of the Powers of Deputies :—

MONTREAL, Oct. 10th, 1878.

To the Supreme Council, 33°, A.·. &° A.·. S.·. Rite, Dominion of Canada.

ILL.·. BRETHREN :

Your Committee to whom was submitted the suggestions of the M.·. P.·. Sov.·. Gr.·. Commander with reference to taking steps to further the propagation of the Rite into places in the Dominion not now occupied, beg to report, that they have considered this important question in all its bearings, and are in entire accord with the ideas expressed, in so far as extending to the Special Deputies for the Provinces the powers therein suggested.

They verily believe the system at present pursued, " that of waiting for Brethren to apply for the Degrees to the nearest Body, and when a sufficient number shall have obtained them to petition for a Warrant" is too tedious a process to warrant in being retained, and therefore if the Rite is to be extended, it is imperatively necessary to have it *introduced* to Brethren, and the *beauties of this system of Masonry* brought to the notice of those of the Craft who may be considered appropriate parties to carry out the desire of this Council.

They therefore recommend, in order to propagate the Rite in places sufficiently large to maintain a Lodge of Perfection, that when a desire has been expressed by a number of Brethren in any City or Town (where the Rite has not previously been established,) for the degrees, with a view to their propagation, the Provincial Deputy of this Council be hereby instructed to go to such place and (selecting only the constitutional number required to form a body of the 14°, including any members of the Rite who may be found in that place,) there and then to confer the degrees up to and including the 16°, charging therefor the sum of $30 to *each Candidate*, after which to report their names and additions, with all particulars to the Secretary General for registration and certificates, and that the said Deputy shall then obtain the petition of these said brethren for a dispensation to open a Lodge of Perfection.

That when the new Lodge is organized, the Supreme Council shall present to it the half of the fees obtained from the members upon whom the Deputy shall have conferred the degrees, in order to form the nucleus of a fund for the furnishing of their Lodge Rooms.

The said Deputy shall render an account of his actual travelling expenses (only), incurred in establishing the said Lodge, and the same having been presented to this Council, and duly audited, shall be paid by an order in the usual course.

Respectfully submitted,

J. W. MURTON, 33°,
Chairman.

On motion of Ill.·. Bro.·. HUTTON, seconded by Ill.·. Bro.·. MURTON, the Rèport was received and adopted.

It was then moved by Ill.·. Bro.·. PETERS, seconded by Ill.·. Bro.·. MURTON, that the Report of the Committee on Foreign Correspondence and Relations be now read again and considered clause by clause.—Carried.

The various clauses of the above named Report, as follows, viz : those referring to the Sup.·. Councils of

The Northern Jurisdiction U. S. A.,
The Southern Jurisdiction U. S. A.,
Mexico,
New Grenada,
Peru,
Brazil,
England,
Scotland,
Belgium,
Switzerland,
Spain,
Egypt,

and the one referring to the Lausanne Confederation, were on motion, after discussion, severally adopted.

The clause referring to a question of Law, submitted by the Sup.·. Co.·. of the Southern Jurisdiction U. S. A., for the consideration of and adoption by sister Supreme Councils as a settled principle of Law of the Ancient and Accepted Scottish Rite, viz :—" That in a Dependency, Province or Colony of a country in which there is a lawful Supreme Council, no foreign power can authorize the creation of a Supreme Council, and a Body so created has no legal existence," was, on motion of Ill.·. Bro.·. PETERS, seconded by Ill.·. Bro.·. MURTON, adopted.

The clause recommending a memorial page in the Proceedings was read, when it was moved by Ill.·. Bro.·. PETERS, seconded by Ill.·. Bro.·. HUTTON, that the Report be adopted, and that the name of Ill.·. Bro.·. VICTOR WALTER, of the Supreme Council of Belgium, be added to those already named.—Carried.

The clause making the recommendation concerning the Supreme Councils of Mexico and New Grenada was, on motion of Ill.·. Bro.·. PETERS, seconded by Ill.·. Bro.·. HUTTON, adopted.

The clause referring to France was then read, when it was moved by Ill.·. Bro.·. PETERS, seconded by Ill.·. Bro.·. HUTTON, and

Resolved, That this clause be adopted, and that this Council, while in full fraternal relations with the Supreme Council for France, has never established fraternal communications with the Grand Orient of France, and will withhold all intercourse with that Grand Orient so long as she persists in a declaration of principles withdrawing from an enunciation of belief in the existence of Almighty God and the immortality of the soul.

It was then moved by Ill.·. Bro.·. PETERS, seconded by Ill.·. Bro.·. REID, that the Report of the Committee on Foreign Correspondence and Relations, be now adopted, and that this Council tender its acknowledgments to the Chairman, Ill.·. Grand Chancellor ELLIS, and the other members of the Committee, for their able report.—Carried.

The following resolution was then passed :—

Moved by Ill.·. Bro.·. HUTTON, seconded by Ill.·. Bro.·. COPELAND, that Ill.·. Bro.·. ———— 32°, ———·— is a fit and proper person to be elected to the rank of the 33rd and last degree of the A.·. & A.·. S.·. Rite, and an active member of this Sup.·. Council.—Carried.

Ill.·. Bro.·. HUTTON then nominated Ill.·. Bro.·. ———— and his name was ordered to be placed on the books of this Sup.·. Council, to be ballotted for at a special session, to be called by the M.·. P.·. Sov.·. Gr.·. Com.·. sometime in the winter, not sooner than January, 1879.

The Committee on Audit and Finance presented the following report :—

To the Supreme Council, 33°, A.·. & A.·. S.·. R.·. for the Dominion of Canada.

Your Committee have audited the accounts of the Secretary and Treasurer General, and find them correct. We find $944.86 cash on hand, and congratulate the Supreme Council on its financial position, due to the zealous manner in which the Secretary and Treasurer have performed their duties.

Respectfully submitted,

ROBERT MARSHALL, 33°,
Chairman.
WM. REID, 33°.

Moved by Ill.·. Bro.·. PETERS, seconded by Ill.·. Bro.·. REID, that the same be received and adopted.—Carried.

The following report, regarding Bro.·. S. G. STRONG, was on motion of Ill.·. Bro.·. MURRAY, seconded by Ill.·. Bro.·. REID, adopted :—

The Committee on the doings of Sub.·. Bodies, to whom was referred the recommendation of Toronto Chapter Rose Croix "That Sov.·. P.·. SAMUEL G. STRONG, 18°, an affiliated member of that Chapter, for the crime of felony, be expelled," beg to report that they have fully considered this unfortunate question and concur in the request of the aforesaid Chapter, and recommend that the said offending brother be expelled from the A.·. & A.·. S.·. Rite, and his name reported to all Councils with whom we are in correspondence.

ROBERT MARSHALL, 33°,
On behalf of the Committee.

Ill.˙. Bro.˙. D. B. TRACY, of the N.˙. J.˙. United States, then addressed the Sup.˙. Council, kindly offering to present this Council with some valuable works, and in the most cordial and fraternal manner extended an invitation to the members of this Council to visit our near neighbors, the Northern Sup.˙. Council of the United States. The Sov.˙. Gr.˙. Com.˙. replied to Ill.˙. Bro.˙. TRACY, thanking him for his kindly offer, that Ill.˙. Brother then retired.

Ill.˙. Bro.˙. MURTON gave notice that at the next annual session of this Council he would move that the Statutes be amended as follows :—That the words on page 10, viz., " from Chapter of Rose Croix, seven dollars," be altered to read, " from Chapter of Rose Croix, covering a Lodge of Perfection and Council of Princes of Jerusalem, seven dollars ; from Chapter of Rose Croix, covering a Council of Princes of Jerusalem, four dollars."

Ill.˙. Bro.˙. HUTTON submitted to the Council a letter from Ill.˙. Bro.˙. COPELAND, explaining the cause of his being absent this day from this Supreme Council.

The Secretary General was instructed to write the absent members of this Council, and send them a copy of the resolution passed at this session, as an addition to the Statutes, referring to absence from the sessions of this Sup.˙. Council.

The Secretary General laid upon the table the Annual Reporter of the Sup.˙. Council of Scotland, and several books of the proceedings of other Supreme Councils, and that officer was directed to record the thanks of this Council, and to supply these Councils regularly with the Proceedings of this Council.

The 31°, as recommended by the Committee on Ritual, was then exemplified, and after a very careful scrutiny was, on motion of Ill.˙. Bro.˙. PETERS, seconded by Ill.˙. Bro.˙.

Reid, adopted as the Ritual of that degree, to be used by all Consistories under this Sup∴ Council.

On motion of Ill∴ Bro∴ Peters, seconded by Ill∴ Bro∴ Murray, the Report of the Committee on Ritual was adopted.

The Sov∴ Grand Commander then appointed the following Standing Committees :—

On Audit and Finance.

Ill∴ Bro∴ Hugh Murray.
" " William Reid.
" " David Ransom Munro.

On Foreign Correspondence and Relations.

Ill∴ Bro∴ John Valentine Ellis.
" " Isaac Henry Stearns.
" " Robert Thomson Clinch.

On Jurisprudence and Legislation.

Ill∴ Bro∴ William Henry Hutton.
" " John Walter Murton.
" " Benjamin Lester Peters.

On Doings of Subordinate Bodies.

Ill∴ Bro∴ Hugh Alexander Mackay.
" " Eugene Mortimer Copeland.
" " Robert Marshall.

On Doings of Inspectors General and Special Deputies.

Ill∴ Bro∴ Hugh Murray.
" " Robert Thomson Clinch.
" " Hugh Alexander Mackay.

On motion, ten dollars was ordered to be handed to Bro∴ ——— for his kind attendance during this session of the Sup∴ Council.

Moved by Ill∴ Bro∴ Peters, seconded by Ill∴ Bro∴ Hutton, that the Secretary General be and is hereby authorized to print five hundred copies of the Proceedings of this session and distribute the same.

Moved by Ill.·. Bro.·. MURRAY, seconded by Ill.·. Bro.·. PETERS, that this Supreme Council desire to express to the members of the Council, resident in Montreal, and to the brethren of that City, their thanks for the very great attention given throughout the session, and for the sumptuous entertainment provided.

The labors of the session being over, the box of fraternal assistance was passed, and the proceeds handed to the Ill.·. Com.·.-in-Chief of Montreal Consistory, for the benevolent fund of that Body.

The chain of union was then formed and the Supreme Council closed its Fifth Session in Peace, Love and Harmony, at six o'clock P. M.

T. D. HARINGTON, 33°,
Sov.·. Gr.·. Commander.

J. W. MURTON, 33°,
   Secretary General H.·. E.·.

Illustrious Brother

JOHN ROBIN MCDANIEL, 33°,

LIEUTENANT GRAND COMMANDER

OF THE SUPREME COUNCIL OF S∴ G∴ I∴ G∴ 33°, FOR THE

Southern Jurisdiction U. S. A.,

For over thirty years an Active Member of the above Illustrious Body.

Illustrious Brother

ORRIN WELCH, 33°,

Active Member and Deputy for the State of New York

OF THE SUPREME COUNCIL OF S∴ G∴ I∴ G∴ 33°, FOR THE

Northern Jurisdiction U. S. A.

Illustrious Brother

UDO SCHLEUSNER, 33°,

ACTIVE MEMBER

OF THE SUPREME COUNCIL OF S.·. G.·. I.·. G.·. 33°,

For Brazil.

Illustrious Brothers

JULES DUCHESNE, 33°,

SECRETARY GENERAL,

AND

—— PACHOUD, 33°,

ACTIVE MEMBER

OF THE SUPREME COUNCIL OF S∴ G∴ I∴ G∴ 33°,

For Switzerland.

Illustrious Brother

Victor Walter, 33°,

ACTIVE MEMBER

OF THE SUPREME COUNCIL OF S∴ G∴ I∴ G∴ 33°,

For Belgium.

APPENDIX.

CONTAINING

LETTERS AND OTHER DOCUMENTS FROM FOREIGN SUPREME COUNCILS
REFERRED TO IN THE FOREGOING PROCEEDINGS, ALSO
SUPPLEMENTAL REPORT OF THE COMMITTEE ON
FOREIGN CORRESPONDENCE AND RELA-
TIONS. ALSO,

TABLEAU

OF THE SUPREME COUNCIL, BODIES UNDER THE SUPREME COUNCIL
AND REGISTERED MEMBERS OF THE RITE IN THE
DOMINION OF CANADA.

Letters and Documents

WHICH WERE REFERRED TO BY THE SOV∴ GR∴ COMMANDER IN HIS
ADDRESS, ALSO IN THE REPORT OF THE COMMITTEE ON FOREIGN
CORRESPONDENCE AND RELATIONS AND SUPPLEMENTAL
REPORT OF THAT COMMITTEE ARE PRINTED FOR
THE INFORMATION OF THE MEMBERS OF
THE RITE IN CANADA.

Circular anent the Ancient and Primitive Rite, issued by the Sov∴ Gr∴ Commander to the Bodies under the obedience of this Sup∴ Council :—

ORDO AB CHAO.

From the East of the Supreme Council of the Sovereign Grand Inspectors General of the 33rd degree of the Ancient and Accepted Scottish Rite of Freemasonry for the Dominion of Canada, under the C∴ C∴ of the Zenith near the B∴ B∴ answering to 45° 23′ N. Lat., and 75° 43′ W. Meridian of Greenwich.

To all to whom these Presents shall come—

HEALTH, STABILITY, WISDOM.

Dear and Ill∴ Bro∴

Information having come to me that certain parties have proposed to establish in this Dominion a system of Freemasonry termed the *"Ancient and Primitive Rite,"* being an abbreviation of that known as the "Rite of Memphis;" such Rite purporting to open Chapters of Rose Croix, and pretending to confer some of the degrees of the *"Ancient and Accepted Scottish Rite;"* and as it appears from an article which was inserted in the Toronto *Mail* newspaper of the 21st May last, that some members of our Obedience are said to be connected with the establishing of the said *"Ancient and Primitive Rite"* in the City of Toronto and elsewhere, and moreover, that they have invited other members of *our Rite* to visit Bodies of their proposed system, thereby inciting them to acts of disobedience in violation of their obligations—as any Bodies, not under this Supreme Council, professing to work any of the degrees of our Rite in this Jurisdiction, must be and are hereby pronounced to be illegal.

Now, therefore, you are hereby directed to call a Special Assembly of your ———— immediately upon receipt of this Circular, and thereat to read the same to the members, as a solemn warning to them, neither to take any part in the establishing of this *new Rite,* nor to hold any fellowship, nor have any masonic intercourse with any member or members of the same on matters touching any of the degrees of the A.˙. & A.˙. S.˙. Rite, under pain of suspension or expulsion ; and lest the reading of this Edict in open ———— should be insufficient to reach the ears of every member of your ————, you are directed to instruct your Registrar or Secretary to prepare a circular note containing the above information, and to send it to each member of your Body, so that all may be made aware of this mandate and be saved from committing, through inadvertance, any act hereby forbidden.

Given under my hand as Sovereign Grand Commander, and the Seal of the Supreme Council, this first day of June, A.D. 1878.

T. D. HARINGTON, 33°,
Sovereign Grand Commander.

Circular letter from Sup.˙. Council of Peru referring to Lausanne Confederation :—

𝔘𝔫𝔦𝔟𝔢𝔯𝔰𝔦 𝔗𝔢𝔯𝔯𝔞𝔯𝔲𝔪 𝔒𝔯𝔟𝔦𝔰 𝔄𝔯𝔠𝔥𝔦𝔱𝔢𝔠𝔱𝔬𝔫𝔦𝔰 𝔞𝔡 𝔊𝔩𝔬𝔯𝔦𝔞𝔪 𝔈𝔫𝔤𝔢𝔫𝔱𝔦𝔰.

ORDO AB CHAO.

Supremo Concejo Confederado del XXXIII y ultimo Grado del Rito Escoces, Antiguo y Aceptado de la Republica del Peru Miembro del Tribunal Instituido por el Tratado de Union y Alianza Celebrado entre los Supremos Concejos Confederados Gr.˙. 33 Or.˙. de Lima, el 13 del 10° Mes Anno Lucis 5877, y el 18 de Deciembre, Anno Vulgo 1877 a los Supremos, Concejos de SS.˙. GG.˙. II.˙. GG.˙. Gr.˙. 33.˙. del rito escoces, Antiguo y Aceptado.

[TRANSLATION.]

M.˙. P. . Sov.˙. Grand Commander, Grand Master and Ill.˙. Brethren.

When the idea was initiated of assembling a Congress of all existing Supreme Councils it was believed with good cause that by this measure perfect harmony would be obtained between all of them, the result of which would be of manifest importance to the Order. Unfortunately experience has proved the contrary : the Confederation of Lausanne has simply been a partial reunion, or

more correctly speaking, was confined to certain Supreme Councils, a very considerable number of said Bodies not attending, and amongst these figure some
which are considered of the highest position.

With this sad disappointment and in order to lessen it's bad effects, a proposal was approved to consider in the number of the Confederated Councils those
who should join the Confederation and should accept its resolutions. There has
not been a single Supreme Council which has joined, nor manifested it's acquies-
cence in these resolutions,—at least the Supreme Council, over which I have the
honour of presiding, has received no official notice that there are more than nine
Supreme Councils which form the Confederation, notwithstanding that this latter
has recognized twenty-two Supreme Bodies of the Ancient and Accepted Scottish
Rite.

The silence of the Supreme Councils which do not form part of the Confederation, the indifference with which some have viewed the resolutions adopted,
the protests of others respecting certain principles sanctioned, and the discontent
of nearly all, eloquently prove that Masonic Congresses are not desirable.

Very different has been the result produced after the Convention of Lausanne ;—the harmony which formerly existed between all the Supreme Councils
has been completely interrupted ;—their intercourse, very close before the Convention, broken off ;—disputes more or less warm have arisen which have given
rise to scandals of some importance ;—without its being possible to avoid the
want of confidence which has existed and which still exists in the bosom of many
of the Supreme Councils.

If such pernicious and fatal consequences are solely to be attributed to the
assembling in Congress of Supreme Councils,—if the hopes have been disap-
pointed of those who deemed the Confederation a means of cementing the relations of these Supreme Bodies, the result of which should redound to the general
welfare of the Order and it's onward progress, if it is our duty to avoid as far as
possible all grounds of disagreement and of inevitable and deep resentment, it is
necessary and indispensable to impede the meeting for the future of any more
Masonic Congresses.

These reasons and many others which will not escape your profound and
enlightened intelligence have impelled the Supreme Council of Peru to request
by means of their Delegates the derogation of the Articles of the Treaty of
Alliance and Confederation, in which has been stipulated the periodical assembling of Masonic Congresses, it being necessary, in the opinion of the Supreme
Council of Peru, that the last should be that which ought soon to be held on the
15th July, 1878, in London.

This derogation being approved, as well as the modifications which it is
necessary to make in the above mentioned Treaty, and which will also be proposed
by said Delegates, harmony will be re-established between all the Councils and
the progress of the Order will be prosperous and happy.

Trusting that the Supreme Council, over which you so worthily preside, will
second these ideas and obtain their approval at the next Congress in London,

pray accept, Illustrious and very dear Brother, the considerations of especial respect of fraternally yours, &c., &c.,

ANTONIO DE SOUZA FERREIRA,

Sov.·. Gr.·. Commander.

RICARDO H. HARTLEY,

Sec.·. Chan.·. Gen.·. of the Order.

Circular letter from Sup.·. Council of Peru, establishing fraternal relations with the Scottish District Grand Lodge:—

[TRANSLATION.]

The Supreme Confederate Council of the 33rd and last Degree of the A.·. & A.·. S.·. R.·. for the Republic of Peru, Member of the Tribunal instituted by the Treaty of Union and Alliance celebrated between the Supreme Confederated Councils 33°.

ORIENT OF LIMA, 18th March, 1878.

Circular No. 1642.

To the Superior Bodies and Symbolic Lodges of the Jurisdiction :

The Supreme Confederate Council of Peru, in view of a Communication directed by the Provincial Grand Lodge of Scotland in Peru, Jurisdiction of the Grand Lodge of Scotland, Orient of Edinburgh, has issued under date 16th inst., the following Resolution :

" Authority is given to the Symbolic Lodges of this Obedience to establish " official and fraternal relations with those of the Provincial Grand Lodge of " Scotland, it being indispensable for the admission of visitors to our Lodges, in " addition to the requisites exacted in the Statutes, to present the Diploma of " Master Mason 3°, issued by the Grand Lodge of Scotland, countersigned and " sealed by the Grand Secretary of the Provincial Grand Lodge of Scotland in " Peru. Members of the Symbolic Lodges and Superior Orders of the Obedience " of the Supreme Confederate Council, in visiting Lodges of the Jurisdiction of the " Provincial Grand Lodge of Scotland, must present their Diplomas of Master " Mason 3°, countersigned and sealed by the Secretary Chancellor General of the " Order. Similar procedure must be observed when Lodges or Superior Bodies " of the Jurisdiction of this Supreme Council are visited by Brethren of the " Obedience, or of other recognized Supreme Bodies from abroad, as the " Decree of 19th January, 1876, prescribes."

I forward you herewith the list of the Lodges under the Jurisdiction of the Grand Lodge of Scotland established at Lima, Callao, Tacna and Mollendo, and will in due time remit you the full account of all the Brethren of the said Jurisdiction who have been expelled from it, and of those who are suspended from their Masonic privileges, in order that they may not be admitted to the Lodge over which you preside.

Accept the cordial and fraternal salute of

Your Brother,

RICARDO H. HARTLEY,

Sec.·. Chan.·. Gen.·. of the Order.

Circular letter from the Sup.·. Council of Colon :—

Supreme Council of Sov.·. Gr.·. Inspectors General of the 33d and last degree of the A.·. & A.·. S.·. R.·. of Freemasonry of Colon for Cuba and the other Islands of the Spanish West Indies, established A. L. 5869. Orient of Santiago de Cuba, under the C.·. C.·. of the Zenith near the H.·. L.·. to the 20° 1′ North Latitude and 69° 40′ Longitude East of the Meridian of San Fernando.

20th Sept., A. L. 5877.

To the Supreme Council for the Dominion of Canada.

CIRCULAR.

VERY DEAR AND ILLUSTRIOUS BRETHREN :

Since the Convention at Lausanne we have on various occasions addressed ourselves to the Confederate Masonic Powers to give them an account of the proceedings at the several sessions held by this Supreme Council, and whether on account of the difficulties which our means of communication presented or those which arose in the addresses of a number of the Sup.·. Confederate Councils which we have not an exact knowledge of, we have observed a want of regularity in replying to our foreign correspondence which in some degree has affected the activity and zeal of our Gr.·. Secy.·. General.

Now that the Postal Treaty of Berne has been proclaimed in this Island we trust that the advantages it affords will prove extensive to this Supreme Council, while avoiding every kind of dullness in its communications.

But as it is necessary to repair the fault of the previously suffered irregularities, we have determined to send the present circular to the friendly Powers to give them an account briefly of the principal actions of this high Body.

In compliance with Article III., paragraph II. of the Grand Constitutions of 1786, revised by the Convention of Lausanne and adopted at its session of 22nd Sept., 1875, this Supreme Council unanimously decided at its session of 23rd April, 1876, to effect its elections of Grand Officers for the space of time marked out in the said article. In consequence, the following Sov∴ Gr∴ Inspectors General were declared elected :—

Ill∴ Bro∴ JUAN MANUEL de la CRUZ,
M∴ Puissant Sov∴ Gr∴ Commander.

"   "   CONSTANTINO INSUA,
Sov∴ Lieut∴ Gr∴ Commander.

"   "   MANUEL JACAS PLA',
Gr∴ Sec∴ Gen∴ Chancellor of the Order.

"   "   L. DE LA BARRERA,
Gr∴ Minister of State, Gr∴ Chaplain.

"   "   FREDK. W. RAMSDEN,
Gr∴ Treas∴ Gen∴ of the Order.

"   "   M. TRIEDN Y. METJE,
Gr∴ Almoner.

"   "   A. R. CAMPINA,
Gr∴ Master of Ceremonies.

"   "   GABRIEL JUNCO,
Gr∴ Standard Bearer.

"   "   A. MIYARES,
Gr∴ Capt∴ of the Guard.

Who, in due time, took possession of their respective offices.

The communication sent to this high body by the Ill∴ Brother who represented it at the Convention of Lausanne and the account rendered of the Proces Verbal, revised Constitutions, Treaty of Union Alliance and Confederation and other resolutions sanctioned by the Universal Congress of Supreme Councils united at the Orient of Lausanne, officially transmitted by the Sup∴ Council of Switzerland, Executive authority of the Confederation, were accepted and promulgated as the only fundamental and General laws of the A∴ & A∴ S∴ R∴ and ordered to be observed by all the high bodies obedient to this Supreme Council.

Nevertheless in ordinary assembly of the 30th April, A. L. 5876, having due respect to the expressed resolutions of the Convent of Lausanne, the following resolution was adopted, which literally read thus : " To accept the " new title of Supreme Council of the 33rd degree of Colon, for Cuba and the " other Islands of the Spanish West Indies, without, by this intending to abdi- " cate the rights that the Supreme Council of Charleston exercised in conceding " to this Supreme Council of Colon when it gave it life, Jurisdiction over the " unoccupied West Indies, which rights it will duly assert."

It was some time after that a grave question threatened the Masonry of Colon with a schism, with a dispute that was resolved to sustain Sym∴ Masonry in revindication of its primitive rites of Sovereignty. And this Sup∴ Council, hearing attentively its reasons, and taking into consideration that its principal object in establishing itself in masonic authority, had been to govern the degrees from the 4th ·to 'the 33rd inclusive, (without prejudice to or renunciation of the rights which is conceded to it by article 8 of the Grand Constitutions of 1786, revised by the Universal Convention of Supreme Councils, united at Lausanne, and adopted at the meeting of 22nd September, 1875,) formulated with the Grand Symbolic Lodge, a Treaty of Friendship and mutual recognition of powers between both Bodies by which that Body was recognized as the sole regular and competent authority to rule and govern in this Jurisdiction of Cuba and the other Islands of the Spanish West Indies, over all regular Symbolic Lodges of A.·. F.·. & A.·. M.·., that work in the three symbolic degrees of apprentice, fellowcraft and master, which treaty it undertook to bring to the knowledge of all Sup.·. Councils and Grand Lodges of its friendship and correspondence.

After this event some dissenters of the Orient of Havana raised the standard of rebellion, communicating to this Supreme Council the establishment of a Grand Symbolic Lodge, styled "Of the Island of Cuba," and requesting that we should establish relations with it; but this high Body, faithful executor of its undertaking, declined to hear such a petition proceeding from fractions of Symbolic offshoots of the Grand Lodge of Colon, rendered insubordinate by petty ambitions which undertook the attempt to usurp some documents, effects and articles of those Symbolic offshoots of the West, believing that the simple occupation of that which they appropriated without being their own, was sufficient to constitute a regular Grand Symbolic Lodge for the Island of Cuba, disavowing the legitimate authority of Colon.

In view of that above manifested, this Supreme Council unanimously resolved to communicate to the Masonic World that the so called Grand Lodge of the Island of Cuba, in the Orient of Havana, is considered by it as a spurious and irregular Body, having risen in rebellion against the legitimate Symbolic authority of Colon for Cuba and the other Islands of the Spanish West Indies, constituted by means of fraud and treason to the true principles of Masonry, and that the only legitimate symbolic authority recognized by this Supreme Council is the most respectable Grand Lodge of Colon for Cuba and the other Islands of the Spanish West Indies.

We deem another incident opportune to make known to universal Masonry, referring to our jurisdiction of the Island of Porto Rico, and it is that, according to advices from that Orient some time ago, there invaded its territory a so called Grand National Orient of Spain or of Calatrava, establishing Symbolic Lodges in several Towns of the Island and a departmental Chapter in the Capital: the Grand National Orient of Venezuela installing the Lodge " Bomiquen," No. 37 of the Orient of San Juan, and the Grand Orient of France constituting the Lodge " Fenix," of the Orient of Ponce.

These occupations cannot subsist any longer, and, we expect it from the consideration of the regular high Bodies, that they consent that in this our

Jurisdiction, sanctioned by the Convention of Lausanne, it works under its auspices as well as of the so called Grand National Orient of Spain, notwithstanding that almost all those of this Obedience have withdrawn their support.

In making this declaration to the Confederate Powers, we beg that they will take it into consideration, ignoring the regularity of any Masonic Body whatever of the Spanish Island of Porto Rico that does not work under the auspices of the Supreme Council, or the Most Respectable Grand Symbolic Lodge of Colon.

We shall conclude by declaring, if we are not wrongly informed, that the Sup.·. Confederate Council, 33°, for the Republic of Uruguay, the Grand Orient of Egypt and Gr.·. Lodge of Italy, recognized and established fraternal relations with the peninsular Schismatic Group enrolled by JUAN A. PEREZ, (Ricardo,) seceding from those that were with JUAN DE LA SOMERA, (obed,) enrolled now with Praixades Mateo Sogasta, considering it as the legitimate Grand Orient for Spain and its Colonial Dependencies.

It is difficult for us to believe that a confederate power can have established a treaty so much at variance with the decisions of the Convention of Lausanne with respect to the Sup.·. Council of Colon, but it is certain that it will redound to the benefit of any high body which through such deplorable error may have become liable to reprehension, and of all who find themselves liable to suffer for it through ignorance of the misfortunes that have afflicted the Order in the jurisdiction of the Spanish Peninsula; if this Supreme Council of Colon raises its voice to throw light on the irregularity of this so called "Grand Orient of Spain and its Colonial Dependencies," which cannot otherwise exist, since the jurisdiction of Cuba and the other Islands of the Spanish West Indies belong to the legitimate Masonry of Colon, and that in Spain there is no other regular Orient, since, by the authority of the Supreme Council of that Jurisdiction, the supporters of that which existed under deed of 15th June, 1874, were overthrown, to which Supreme Council, of our friendship and recognition, belong the right to exercise authority over all degrees of the Order in Spain, as it gave due notice thereof, and as we so understand it.

Since that date the title of Grand Orient has been, and is in Spain the exclusive patrimony of the Schismatic fractions, appropriating to themselves simultaneously that which was presided over by Calatrava and by Somera, and which is now that of Sagasta, JUAN A. PEREZ, and others whom we do not remember.

That which we undertake to expose, will give to universal Masonry an idea of the confusion which reigns in the Spanish Peninsula since legitimate Masonry closed the doors to personal ambitions, so long as the opinion of the Masonic World shall judge and decide the road it had to pursue in advance.

We hope and recommend the Supreme Confederate Councils may devote themselves with preferable attention to this subject at the next Convention of

1878, giving to disturbed Spain, our Mother Country, a legitimate representation in the Universal Masonic Congress.

We salute you, dear and Illustrious Brethren, offering you our fraternal affection and our highest consideration.

(Signed)   JUAN MANUEL DE LA CRUZ, 33°,

Sov∴ Gr∴ Com∴

(Signed)   MANUEL JACAS PLA',

Gr∴ Sec∴ Gen∴ Chan∴ of the Order.

Circular letter from Sup∴ Council of San Domingo, with Tableau of its Officers and Members :—

[TRANSLATION.]

SUPREME COUNCIL OF SOV∴ GR∴ INS∴ GENERAL FOR THE REPUBLIC OF DOMINIQUE, ORIENT OF SAN DOMINGO.

1st June, 1878.

To the M∴ Ill∴ Sov∴ Gr∴ Commander of the Supreme Council of Canada :

We have the honor to forward enclosed for your cognizance and consequent purposes the roll of the Officers and Members who compose this Supreme Council.

We beg that you will have the kindness to be our Representative near the High Body you so worthily preside over, making known to it that we raise our fervent prayers to the G∴ A∴ O∴ T∴ U∴ for its prosperity.

We salute you fraternally

(Sd.)   LUCAS GIBBES, 33°

Gr∴ Sec∴ Gen∴

List of Grand Officers elected by this Sup∴ Com∴ for the Quadrennial from 27th February, 1878 to 27th February, 1882, in Grand Assembly, 5th May, 1878, and of the rest of the active members of the same.

JACINTO DE CASTRO,	*Sov∴ Gr∴ Com∴*
JOSE DE CASTRO,	*Lieut∴ " Com∴*
NOEL HENRIQUES,	" *Minister of State.*
LUCAS GIBBES,	*Sec∴*
SANTIAGUO GERALDINO,	" *Treasurer.*
PEDRO A. DELGADO,	" *Registrar.*
MARTIN RODRIGUEZ,	" *Mas∴ of Cer∴*
APOLINAR DE CASTRO,	·· *Expert.*
PEDRO M. PINEIRO,	" *Almoner.*
GEORGE MANSFIELD,	" *Standard Bearer,*
EXEQUIEL MEDINA,	" *Sword* "
FEDERICO RAMIREZ,	" *Capt∴ of Guard.*

ACTIVE MEMBERS—SULLY DuBREIL, &c., &c., &c.

DELEGATES OF THE SUP∴ COUN∴ IN THE PROVINCES OF THE CIBAO.— RAFAEL M. LEYBA, &c., &c., &c.

Circular letter from the Supreme Council of Spain :—

The Supreme Council of Sov.·. Gr.·. Inspectors General of the 33rd and last degree of the A.·. & A.·. S.·. R.·. of Freemasons for the Jurisdiction of Spain, established A.·. L.·. 5811, under the C.·. C.·. of the Z.·. near the H.·. L.·. to the degrees 40° 24' 57 N. Lat. and to the degrees 0° 1' Lon. E. of the Meridian of Madrid.

6th May, 1878.

To the Supreme Confederate Council for Canada at Ottawa.

VERY DEAR AND ILLUSTRIOUS BRETHREN :

Trusting in the justice of the Universal Congress of the Supreme Councils of the 33rd and last degree of the A.·. & A.·. S.·. R.·. convoked at London, we await the decision on the demand for recognition and admission amongst the number of the Confederates which this Council, legally constituted on the 4th July, 1811, for the Jurisdiction of Spain, had the honor to present to the Convent of Lausanne. In the meantime we must address you these presents which will complete the grounds of the desired decision, with a succinct account of the events which have transpired in this Supreme Council since the communication which its Sov.·. Gr.·. Commander Nephtali addressed to that of Switzerland under date of 25th June, 1876, which ought also to operate towards the above-mentioned demand.

That Sov.·. Gr.·. Commander was relieved from his labours here on earth in he 86th year of his age ; the G.·. & Sup.·. Arch.·. of the Universe had the goodness to call him to his bosom on the 7th day of August, 1877.

The Supreme Council reunited in extraordinary session, by reason of this sad event, on the 17th day of the same month ; the Convocation unanimously decided on its reorganization, for such time as the Ill.·. Deputy Gr.·. Com.·. should deem necessary, to try to bring before the tribunal of Sov.·. Gr.·. Inspectors General of this Jurisdiction, in which the office of Sov.·. Gr.·. Com.·. must be vested in accordance with the Constitutions and Statutes of 1786, to them who boasting the 33° in the various Schismatic Groups, should possess it legitimately and will respond to the call, accepting the integrity and loyal observance of the dogmas, doctrines, institutes and constitutions of the Order in which only can truth and fraternal union exist, which was desired by this Sup.·. Council. The Representative of the Supreme Council of Colon, Ill.·. Bro.·. LEANDRO TOMAS PASTOR, declared that this decision was in accordance with certain indication he had received from the said Supreme Council, and could not be less than agreeable to all the other Sovereign bodies of the degree.

On the 5th of December this Supreme Council met in special session, convoked by the Ill.·. Deputy Grand Commander, in order to place before it a communication (Baluster) from Sov.·. Gr.·. Insp.·. General GRAVINA, member of the Sup.·. Co.·. of Colon, which Sovereign Power had regularly conferred upon him the 33rd degree at the meeting of the 21st March, 1869. By this communication he made known that he had taken up his residence at Madrid, and requested that he should be inscribed on the roll of Sovereign Grand Inspectors General of this Jurisdiction as one of the members of its Supreme Council.

For this purpose he enclosed with said communication another from the Sup. ∴ Council of Colon, conceding him the necessary authority according to Article 15 of the Treaty of Union, Alliance and Confederation of the Supreme Councils of the A. ∴ & A.∴ S.∴ R.∴ executed at Lausanne, 22nd Sept., 1875.

With the customary solemnities, the Ill.∴ Bro. ∴ GRAVINA was received, and took his seat as an ordinary member of this Supreme Council.

After due citation to all Sov.∴ Gr.∴ Inspectors General of the Jurisdiction of Spain, the Tribunal of the same was Constituted on the 2nd May, 1878. The Ill. ∴ Dep.∴ Gr.∴ Com.∴ said he was sorry to say that his continued and fraternal exertions, made by virtue of the decision of the 17th August, 1877, had produced no other result than the painful convictions that upon none of the many who boasted the 33° in the Schismatic groups had it been conferred in Supreme Council, neither regularly nor irregularly constituted, with the exception of those who had been expelled from the Order by the Sup.∴ Council of Spain, by means of competent process, and that these as well as the others had repelled all calls to order, doggedly maintaining the punishable error that masonry had no other object than the mission of violence in religious and political questions.

Subsequently the same Ill.∴ Dep.∴ Gr.∴ Com.∴ CINCINATO took the regulation oath of the Office of Sov.∴ Gr.∴ Com.∴, which by the death of the eminent and aged NEPHTALI, of venerated memory, the 2nd paragraph of Article 3 of the Constitutions and Statutes of 1786, marked him for. He took the seat of his rank and proceeded to the re-organization of the Supreme Council, which resulted in manner following :

Ill.∴ Dep.∴ Gr.∴ Com.∴ - - - .	CATON DE UTICA.
Gr.∴ Sec.∴ Gen.∴ - - - - -	MOISES.
Ill.∴ Minister of State, - - - -	PORLIER.
Gr.∴ Mas.∴ of Cer.∴ - - - - ∴	ALLAN KARDEC.
Gr.∴ Capt.∴ of the Guard, - - -	CARLOS XII.
Gr. Chan.∴ - - - - - -	BEZALEEL.
Gr.∴ Treas.∴ - - - - -	ARIG.
Gr. Standard Bearer, - - - -	ARGUELLES,

Who took possession of their respective Offices.

In continuation, the Gr.∴ Sec.∴ General stated that as such, and as Represent-ative of the Sup.∴ Council of Colon, which being one of the Confederates, was at the Convention of Lausanne and would be at the next at London, the patron of the claims of Spain to be recognized and admitted to the Confederation, he would remind it that as it appears from the Proceedings and as communicated to the Executive Authority of the Convention, under date 25th July, 1876, he had accepted opportunely and with due solemnities the Grand Revised Con-stitutions, the Treaties of Union, Alliance and Confederation, and all the other resolutions sanctioned by the Universal Congress of Sup.∴ Councils 33° united at Lausanne at its Session of 22nd September, 1875. That by virtue of this acceptance it had to reorganize itself conformably to the disposition in Article 3, paragraph 2, of the said Gr.·. Constitutions, and that this had not been done owing to the intensity of the sufferings of the memorable Sov.·. Gr.·. Com.·. NEPHTALI, and since his death for the reasons which convened the actual reorganization of the Council, considered necessary to the end that the proceed· ing of conformity with the above ·cited article might be effected by virtue of a decision regularly taken by the Sup.·. Council.

In the hearing of this Sov.·. Body were read the proceedings and a record of the communication to which the Gr.·. Sec.·. Gen ·. had referred. Likewise were read the Gr.·. Constitutions, revised by the Convention, comparing them, article by article, with the original text. The Ill.·. Dep.·. Gr.·. Com.·. com· mented on and proved with luminous explanations the amendments made by the Convention, and the resolution of his acceptance was with absolute unanimity and with all solemnity confirmed and ratified. Likewise was confirmed and rati· fied with absolute unanimity the resolution of acceptance of the Treaties of Union, Alliance and Confederation, and all the other resolutions adopted by the Convention, and sanctioned at its Session of the 22nd Sept., 1875.

In consequence of the preceding ratifications and in compliance with Article 3, paragraph 2, of the said Gr.·. Constitutions of 1786, revised by the Convent of Lausanne, this Supreme Council resolved to effect its Elections of Gr.·. Officers for the space of time pointed out in the same Article. This resolution being adopted, they suspended their labours to continue them on the fifth day of the same month.

Having been constituted on this day, the Tribunal of Sov ·. Gr.·. Inspectors General ratified and confirmed the proceedings of the previous meeting, and in compliance with its last resolution proceeded with due solemnity to the Election of Grand Officers of this Supreme Council, and the following Sov.·. Gr.·. Inspectors General were declared elected.

For M.·. Puissant Sov.·. Gr.·. Commander,	ILL. BRO.	GRAVINA.
" Sov.·. Lieut.·. Gr.·. Commander, -	" "	CATON DE UTICA.
" Sec.·. Gen.·. Chancellor of the Order,	" "	MOISES.
" Gr.·. Minister of State, Gr.·. Chaplain,	" "	CINCINATO.
" Gr.·. Treasurer Gen.·. of the Order,	" "	ARIG.
" Gr.·. Almoner, - - - .	" "	BEZALEEL.
" Gr.·. Master of Ceremonies, - -	" "	ALLAN KARDEC.
" Standard Bearer, - - - -	" "	ARGUELLES.
" Capt.·. of the Guard, - - -	" "	CARLOS XII.

Who took possession of their respective Offices.

Subsequently this Supreme Council confirmed and ratified all the resolutions adopted by the same in its previous form and organization, in so far as they should not be contrary to the Grand Revised Constitutions and other resolutions of the Universal Congress of Supreme Councils of the 33rd Degree united at Lausanne, which they commanded should be solemnly promulgated throughout all the Bodies of the Obedience of this Supreme Council, and faithfully observed by the same as the fundamental and general laws of the A.˙. & A.˙. S.˙. Rite, to the abolition of all others in so far as they were not in conformity with them.

Finally, it resolved that all the aforesaid acts and resolutions should be made known to the Executive Authority of the Convention and to the other Supreme Confederate Councils.

And in compliance with this resolution we have the honour to communicate to you these presents, praying that the Almighty may grant us your good-will, and may enlighten you and preserve you in his holy keeping.

GRAVINA, °33
Sov.˙. Gr.˙. Commander.

CATON DE UTICA, 33°
Sov.˙. Lt.˙. Gr.˙. Commander.

MOISES, 33°
Gr.˙. Sec.˙. Gen.˙. Chancellor.

Circular letter from the Supreme Council of Switzerland relating to Sup.˙. Council of Peru and the Lausanne Confederation :—

THE SUPREME COUNCIL OF THE 33° FOR SWITZERLAND, (EXECUTIVE AUTHORITY FOR THE CONFEDERATION OF SCOTTISH MASONIC POWERS.)

Orient of Lausanne, 2nd August, 1878.

The Sup.˙. Com.˙. of the 33° of the A.˙. & A.˙. S.˙. R.˙. for Switzerland, by its Sov.˙. Grand Commander.

To the T.˙. P.˙. Supreme Council, of the same Degree for Canada.

T.˙. P.˙. Sov.˙. Gr.˙. Com.˙. T.˙. Ill.˙. Inspectors General :

The Supreme Council of Switzerland, Executive Authority of the Confederation of the Sovereign Powers of the Scottish Rite allied by the Treaty of 22nd September, 1875, has been strangely surprised at the Peruvian Circular of the 18th of December last.

If the Brethren of Peru would only believe it, experience would have shown that it was a mistake to suppose that by means of a Congress perfect union could be created amongst all the Bodies of the Scottish Rite. We would be in presence of a sad deception, which the Convent would have endeavored to connive at, in adopting the idea, however natural and logical, of considering as forming part of the Confederation, the Supreme Councils which might adhere to the resolutions of Lausanne.

The Supreme Council of Peru does not fear to allege, before being informed, that there is not a single Supreme Council which may have given its adhesion to the decisions of the Convent of 1875.

Then our Ill.·. Brethren of Peru describe the pretended silence of the Supreme Councils, still outside the alliance, the indifference of some, the protests of others concerning certain principles admitted at Lausanne, but without stating which, and the discontent of nearly all.

According to Peru the Convent of Lausanne would have the effect of weakening the union which previously existed among all the Supreme Councils; of destroying it among some, without naming them, and of occasioning discussions, more or less violent, calculated to cause very serious scandals, and to excite distrust among the many Bodies of the Scottish Rite.

They take good care not to tell where, for what precise cause, or among what members of the alliance such an afflicting result of the Lausanne Congress would be produced.

And after these visionary considerations, without stating (to serve them for base or pretext) any serious facts in support of this vehement vituperation of the work of Convents; the Supreme Council of Lima declares it necessary and indispensable to prevent, in the future, the meeting of new Masonic·Congresses.

Certainly after such preliminary remarks, it was easy to foresee the decision which would be taken at Lima, to propose, at the time of the meeting of the Convent at London, the suppression of the articles of the Treaty of Union, Alliance and Confederation, which institute the periodical meetings of Masonic Congresses.

The organ of the Universal Clerico-political reaction would have concluded differently against the Federation created at Lausanne.

In beholding a member of the alliance denounce *urbi et orbi* the inauspicious influence of Masonic Congresses, and preach abstention, our irreconcilable enemies ought to rejoice, and follow with lively interest such efforts to divide this Masonic Society, whose moral power they dread.

Did our Illustrious Brethren of Peru well reflect that by their lamentable circular they were going to bring upon themselves the approbation of the fanatic propagators of the anti-social doctrines of the Vatican?

Have we not to fear that some hidden influence, under deceptive appearances, may be insinuated into the bosom of certain Scottish Rite Bodies? for we remark the same symptom in Canada and the same in Italy.

This is why we adjure you, Ill.·. Brethren of Peru, to again weigh well your resolutions, and to ask you again if it is for the interest of the Scottish Rite to submit them at the next Congress.

Is it not singular that in Peru and Canada they open a campaign against Confederation and Congresses, at the very time that our direst enemy, Clericalism, since we must call it by its name, organizes with the greatest strength a formidable contest against Freemasonry : against the liberties conferred by the people after ages of sufferings of all kinds, and at the price of bloody sacrifices !

Might not this be a serious indication that the Devil seeks to insinuate him-self into our ranks ?

We, the Executive Authority of Confederation, guardian of the Supreme Authority, with which we have been invested by a special favor from our dear and Illustrious allies until the next convent, here declare, that we cannot permit disuniting criticisms on the legitimate influence of Congresses for the progress of Scottish Masonry to circulate without our energetic protest.

Of all the members of the Alliance up to the present, Peru only has uttered a discordant note from beyond the sea, at the beginning of an undertaking to which time only can give consecration by demonstrating its happy fruitfulness and assuring its development for the great benefit of Scottish Masonry in both worlds.

Alone, we say, the Supreme Council of Peru appears to give up the collective mission we have given ourselves, before a serious and sufficient experience can have proved whether Convents are an innovation, useless and injurious to the Order.

Whence then can it derive its motives for discouragement ? when it was the object of a flattering and coveted distinction at the Convent of Lausanne, by its admission to a seat at the Federal Tribunal.

We cannot have the fears formulated at Lima, and we hope they will find little echo in Europe, if it is not there where that hidden influence, denounced above, might have penetrated.

We must hope that this trifling cloud, formed over there in the extreme west, will be dispersed and will not carry the storm with it into the midst of the next Conference which sits at London or Rome ; we have firm belief of it.

If the Convent at Lausanne has at first joined together only nine Supreme Councils, whose fault is it ? but the proof of the vitality and the future that is assured to it, is, that since the proclamation of the resolutions of that first Convent, eight other Supreme Scottish Authorities have spontaneously adhered, and requested entrance to the Confederation.

Let us add that quite recently a similar adhesion has come from Madrid, on the part of the two Bodies which dispute supremacy.

The Ill.·. Brethren of Peru will be willing to confess that this is an assuredly delightful success at the end of less than three years—17 out of 22   They are then unhappy in preaching abstention, especially after the glorious defeat of the attempt at plot of the few separatists at Edinburgh.

The Alliance was freely and enthusiastically concluded, and the subsequent adhesions, upon which the next Convent will decide, were spontaneous ; but if they repent of this generous impulse to Confederation, they should come to the next Congress to make known the motives which determine them to re-enter an isolated state.

No one would think of bringing pressure to bear to retain them against their will in the Chain of Union, whatever regret their estrangement would cause us.

To fight the good fight we do not want lukewarm comrades seized with discouragement before the struggle, without a firm faith in victory, and who would like to reap without labour, and triumph without having fought.

To the Convent of Lausanne have adhered since that time those Supreme Councils whose high influence was most important to success, that is, those whom public opinion places really in the first rank ; we may mention England, France, Belgium, &c.

With these powerful elements of strength and prosperity we can without presumption trust in the future of the Scottish Association, and expect with confidence that, better convinced by experience, those who doubt to-day will arrive at a more just appreciation of periodical meetings of Supreme Councils. They will all wish to add by their knowledge, to the *eclat* of the Convent of 1879; and those who might be separated from their valley with the resolution to oppose it will rally under the Federal Banner. This is our prayer.

In the meantime the Executive Authority should raise itself with force against the assertion that Convents are unfavorable to the progress of Scottish Masonry, to the harmony in its midst.

Ah ! the Clericals do not judge this of them. The Supreme Council of Switzerland does not know to what grave conflicts between actual members of the Alliance Peru makes allusion. It has not received any communication on this subject, and if in the meantime a serious difference had arisen on some part of the Earth between Confederates, would it not have been their first duty to inform us of it in order to intervene with a view to conciliation, or to prepare a report on the question for the next Congress, and to enquire upon whom the responsibility of this trouble should rest.

Should it not be rather to the Scottish Authorities still outside of the Alliance, or those preoccupied with having certain religions adopted without the great principles proclaimed at Lausanne, that the quarrels vaguely hinted at in the circular of Peru, should be attributed, instead of imputing them a *priori* without examination or proof to the Congress of 1875 ?

Up to this day we have only heard in the midst of the Confederation, the isolated voice of Peru crying out about deception, and pretending that there is not a single Confederate Council which submits to the resolutions of Lausanne.

We do not know any of them who may have violated their plighted faith ; but if there were any who might consider the Treaty of Alliance a dead letter, they should be judged.

Before risking such an affirmation, should not the Supreme Council of Lima point out to us plainly these conflicts, indicate their cause, and name the authorities in conflict ?

Where then is the proof of the indifference, discontent, and distrust that our Illustrious Brethren of Peru perceive, as they say, all over the world.

Until proof to the contrary, we shall remain persuaded that almost all the Allied Bodies have faith in the efficacy of the Association and Congresses.

If Union causes strength in profane enterprises, ought it not with greater reason have the same effect in Freemasonry. By Association only can we obtain great results ; and it is not at the end of two years of existence that complaint should be made that the Alliance may not yet have produced all the benefits hoped for by its promoters.

How could there be established a true solidaity and a universal law to insure its application, abuses be repressed, conflicts be appeased, infringements on the jurisdiction of each supreme authority be prevented, and ameliorations demonstrated by experience be introduced, if periodical meetings were proscribed, if each wished to live and labour in isolation ?

Is it alienation of independence to enter into a confederacy in order to follow a common law, and impress on our institution a regular and permanent action ?

We maintain then that the idea of convoking in Convent all recognized legitimate Supreme Councils was a happy inspiration. And far from weakening the harmony and cordiality of the relations between them, similar periodical meetings, in which the chief dignatories come to exchange their ideas and learn to understand each other, can only strengthen the ties which unite them, and excite the emulation of all, without any great injury to the independence necessary to each Supreme Council to move in the sphere of its own charter. That is why we oppose with all our might the opinion put forth by Peru concerning Congresses.

The Freemason, supported by hope in his trials, ought to distinguish himself by faith in his work and perseverance in his labour.

Let us take example. from the associations for profane, political, religious, industrial or benevolent purposes, and admire the fruitful results they arrive at if wisdom direct them.

Let us behold above all to what fabulous power the most redoubtable association, that which has the Syllabus for Gospel, has arrived ; and then let each of us, interrogating his conscience and reason, ask himself if renouncing federation and periodical Congresses would not be to sacrifice, with fickle heart, to the secular enemy of Freemasonry one of the most efficacious means for the progress of the Scottish Rite, and for the accomplishment of our task in that struggle engaged in to the utmost, in the old world especially, between reaction and liberty, between liberal thinkers and the advocates of Divine Right of absolutism, under all its forms, to cause humanity to retrograde, and to put it into this new bed of Procrustus, like unto a shirt of violence — the Syllabus ?

Could it be permitted us in the nineteenth century, under the fallacious pretext of occupying ourselves with neither religion nor politics, to indemnify ourselves for this gigantic struggle against the " old man " in both hemispheres, by taking refuge in fictions and abstract platonic contemplations ?

Let us then be in the ranks to bar the passage to this clerico-political Camorra, which endeavours to revive an irrevocably condemned past. It is not to fight there for a political party but for the emancipation of man in order that he may accomplish his destiny.

Let our rallying cry always be "Alliance, solidarity, God and our rights as free men."

T∴ P∴ Sov∴ Gr∴ Com∴ and T∴ Ill∴ Inspectors General, it is with this hope which fortifies us, with this faith which calls us to the fray, that we address to you the most fraternal salutations, with the heartiest prayers that the G∴ A∴ O∴ T∴ U∴ may protect and bless our labours.

In the name and by the command of the Supreme Council of Switzerland, executive authority of the Confederation.

(Signed,)   A. AMBERNY, 33°,
Sov∴ Gr∴ Com∴

(Signed,)   J. DELACRETAZ, 30°,
Asst∴ Gr∴ Sec∴ Gen∴

Circular referring to the adjournment of the meeting of the Confederated Councils which was to have taken place at London, this year :—

THE SUPREME COUNCIL, 33°, FOR SWITZERLAND, (EXECUTIVE AUTHORITY OF THE CONFEDERATION OF THE SCOTTISH MASONIC POWERS,)

ORIENT OF LAUSANNE, 20th May, 1878.

The Sup∴ Coun∴ of the 33° of the A∴ & A. S. R. for Switzerland, by the Sov∴ Gr∴ Com∴ to the T∴ P∴ Sup∴ Council of the same Degree for Canada.

T∴ P∴ Sov∴ Gr∴ Com∴ and T∴ Illustrious Brethren :

Political events having determined the Supreme Council of England to propose the postponement for at least twelve months of the meeting of the next Convent, we hasten to adhere to the wish of our very dear and Illustrious English Brethren.

We have recognized the opportuneness of this adjournment ; in consequence, our Circular of 28th July, 1877, convening you at London on the 15th July next, must be considered as of no effect.

Next year, and in good time, the Supreme Council for Switzerland, Executive Authority of the Confederation established at Lausanne in 1875, will address you a new Circular, fixing the date and place where the Convent will sit.

Let us pray, T∴ Ill∴ Brethren, in the interests of humanity, that peace may be re-established in the east, and that at the next Convent we may all be enabled to labour with complete liberty of mind to the advancement of the reign of Masonic principles among all men.

Accept, T∴ P∴ Sov∴ Gr∴ Com∴ and T∴ Ill∴ Brethren, the expression of our most devoted and-fraternal feelings.

> J. A. AMBERNY, 33°, Sov∴ Gr∴ Com∴
>
> JULES DUCHESNE, 33°, Gr∴ Sec'y.
>
> J. DELACRETAZ, 30°, Ass't Sec'y.

Circular of the Supreme Council of England and Wales regarding the Grand Orient of France :—

Universi Terrarum Orbis Architectonis ad Gloriam Ingentis.

ORDO AB CHAO.

From the East of the Supreme Council of the Sovereign Grand Inspectors General of the 33rd degree of the Ancient and Accepted Rite of Freemasonry for England and Wales and the Dependencies of Great Britain under the C∴ C∴ of the Zenith near the B∴ B∴ answering to 51° 30' N. Lat., and 6' W. Meridian of Greenwich.

To the M∴ P∴ Sov∴ G∴ Cr∴ of the Supreme Council, 33°, for Canada.

RESOLUTION passed by the Supreme Council, 33°, for England, Wales, and the Dependencies of the British Crown, on Wednesday, the 7th November, 1877 :—

Whereas the Grand Orient of France confers Masonic Degrees from the Fourth to the Eighteenth Degree and upwards ;

And whereas at their meeting held on the 13th day of September, 1877, they have declared it to be unnecessary to require of Candidates for admission into Freemasonry a declaration of their belief in the existence of God, the Great Architect of the Universe ;

And whereas this Supreme Council holds such a declaration to be a necessary condition of admission into Freemasonry ; and further, that no person can be legitimately regarded as a Freemason unless he doth declare his belief in Almighty God ;

It is resolved that this Supreme Council, 33°, does from henceforth cease to hold any alliance or Masonic intercourse with the Grand Orient of France, and does hereby instruct and direct its Subordinate Bodies to hold no communion in the Degrees of the Ancient and Accepted Rite, from the 4° to the 33° inclusive, with the Members of the various bodies established by, or owing allegiance to, the said Grand Orient.

And it is ordered that a copy of this Resolution be forwarded to the Grand Orient of France, as also to all Supreme Councils, 33°, with which this Supreme Council is in fraternal alliance, for their general information ; and further, that notification of the same be forthwith transmitted to all the Subordinate Bodies holding under, and bearing allegiance to, this Supreme Council, 33°, in order that the decision herein recorded may come into full force and execution without delay.

Certified to be a true Copy.

SHADWELL H. CLERKE, 33°,

Gd.·. Secretary General,
Supreme Council of England, Wales, and the
Dependencies of the British Crown.

33 GOLDEN SQUARE,
22nd November, 1877.

Circular of the Supreme Council of Ireland regarding the Grand Orient of France :—

𝔇ei 𝔒ptimi 𝔐aximi 𝔘niversitatis 𝔕erum 𝔉ontis ac 𝔒riginis ad 𝔊loriam.

SUPREME COUNCIL OF THE 33RD DEGREE FOR IRELAND.

To the Sov.·. Gr.·. Inspectors General ; to the Representatives of the Council of the 33rd Degree for Ireland near the Masonic Authorities of our Correspondence ; and to all Masonic Bodies of our Obedience.

The S.·. G.·. Commander of the Council of the 33rd Degree of the Ancient and Accepted Rite for Ireland, on behalf of that Council, sends Greeting :

ILL.·. AND DEAR BRETHREN,

The Grand Orient of France, which is the Governing Body of the Degrees of Blue Masonry in France and the French Possessions, claims to have under its obedience several Bodies of the Higher Grades of the above mentioned Rite.

Previously to the 13th September, 1877, the Grand Orient of France recognized certain Constitutions of Freemasonry, the first Article whereof declared the Principles of Freemasonry to be the Existence of God, the Immortality of the Soul, and human solidarity (*solidarite humaine*).

It is plain that a professed Atheist or Materialist could not, consistently with hat Constitution be admitted a Freemason. But the Grand Orient of France, on the 13th September, 1877, altered that Article, and now declares the Principles of Masonry to be "absolute liberty of conscience and human solidarity."

This change seems to us of great importance. For as the Grand Orient does not now declare that a belief in God or in a future life is a recognized principle of Freemasonry, but has deliberately announced its absolute indifference to all opinions, it follows that it does not now hold the profession of Atheism or Materialism would disqualify any person from becoming a Freemason. But we hold and have ever held it to be an essential, universal and unalterable Principle of Freemasonry, that every one initiated therein must profess his faith in Almighty God, and believe in a future existence and the moral responsibility of man.

Whatever was the intention of the alteration above mentioned, the result may be, and is likely to be, that persons who do not believe in God or in a future life will become Masons ; and an original Rule of our Fraternity, which we are bounden in duty as well as inclination to observe and uphold, may thus be rendered of none effect.

Having seriously considered these matters at a Session of our Supreme Council, holden on the 21st day of January, 1878, we have, however reluctantly, resolved as follows :

First.—That this Supreme Council doth from henceforth suspend and cease to hold Masonic communication with the Grand Orient of France.

Secondly.—That all Masonic Bodies subordinate to our jurisdiction be, and they are hereby admonished, until further order of this Council, not to hold Masonic communication with the Grand Orient of France or any person of its jurisdiction.

Thirdly.—That copies of these Resolutions be sent to the several Representatives of this Council, that they may communicate the same to the Powers near which they are accredited : and that copies thereof be also sent to the several Masonic Bodies of our Obedience.

Wherefore we have sent to you this letter, hereby enjoining the Bodies of our Obedience that the same be read aloud in each such Body at its meeting next after the receipt hereof.

And so we bid you farewell. May our Father in Heaven have you in His holy keeping.

Given under my hand and the Seal of our Supreme Council, at Dublin, in Ireland, this 26th day of January, 1878, V∴E∴, in the 51st year of our Council.

J. F. TOWNSHEND, 33°,
S. G. Commander.

Circular of the Supreme Council of England and Wales regarding the Supreme Council of Egypt, with copy of correspondence between the Sup∴ Co∴ of England and that of Italy :—

33 GOLDEN SQUARE, LONDON, W., 1878.

DEAR SIR AND ILL∴ BROTHER,—

I am directed by the Supreme Council, 33°, for England, Wales, and the Dependencies of the British Crown, to bring before your Supreme Council, as a Member of the Confederated Councils, for their serious consideration, the following case, which appears to this Supreme Council to be directly in contravention of the Treaty of Alliance made at Lausanne, in September, 1875, and to express a hope that the Supreme Council of Egypt may not be recognized by any of the Members of the Confederation, without the general assent of that Body.

As the correspondence between this Supreme Council and that of Italy (Turin) fully explains the case, I offer no comment upon it, but merely ask the earnest attention of your Supreme Council to the letters appended hereto.

I have the honor to be,

Dear Sir and Ill∴ Brother,

Yours fraternally,

HUGH D. SANDEMAN, 33°,

Gr∴ Sec∴ Foreign Correspondence.

To the Grand Secretary General,
    Supreme Council, 33°, for Canada.

33, GOLDEN SQUARE, LONDON, W.,
3rd May, 1878.

DEAR SIR AND ILL∴ BRO∴

The Sovereign Grand Commander of the Supreme Council of the Southern Jurisdiction of the United States of America has informed us that "The Supreme Council of Egypt, of which Ill∴ Bro∴ Zola is Sovereign Grand Commander, having been reorganized by the Supreme Council of Italy at Turin, by a Member of the latter Council especially commissioned to that effect," has invited his Council to "enter into relations with it of correspondence and amity."

I am instructed to inquire whether the above statement by the so-called Supreme Council of Egypt is correct, as under Art. V. of the Treaty of Alliance such a step could not legally be taken " without first consulting the other confederated Councils and obtaining a majority of votes in its favour."

I may add that this Supreme Council of Egypt was created by a Body calling itself the Supreme Council of Palermo, which, as you may recollect, asked to be recognized by the Congress of Lausanne in 1875, and was refused.

I am, &c.,

(Signed)   HUGH D. SANDEMAN, 33°,

Gr∴ Sec∴ Foreign Correspondence.

To Ill∴ Bro∴ LA SALLE,
  Sec∴ Gen∴ Sup∴ Co∴, Italy.

[TRANSLATION.]

TURIN, 19th May, 1878.

To∴ Ill∴ Bro∴ HUGH D. SANDEMAN,
  Gr∴ Sec∴ Foreign Cor∴ Supreme Council of England, London.

DEAR SIR AND T∴ ILL∴ BROTHER :

I have the honor to reply to your favour of the 3rd upon the legality and regularity of the Supreme Council of Egypt.

Without doubt the decision of the Delegates of Supreme Councils at the Convent of Lausanne (session of the 7th September, 1875) not to recognize the Supreme Council of Palermo as Supreme legal Authority, was in conformity with Article 5, sec. 3 of the General Statutes of 1786 ; but it could not prevent the Supreme Council of Italy sitting at Turin, from making arrangements to convert it into one of its sections for the Masonic Jurisdiction of the Island of Sicily with-headquarters at Palermo.

When Italy was divided into several States, Italian Masonry was also divided into several Grand Bodies more or less irregular and independent of one another, and in order to unite them in a common masonic bond under the obedience of the Supreme legal Authority, it was necessary to act towards them with much prudence and consideration so as not to wound their self-love and susceptibility.   That is the reason the Supreme Council of Turin in its capacity of Sole Supreme and legal Authority for all Italy, has felt it its duty to recognize the actions the said Grand Bodies had performed.

Now, as the Supreme Council of Egypt had been constituted by that of Palermo before the Congress of Lausanne, the Supreme Council of Turin was logically obliged to recognize it in its turn, and it is for this reason that it has delegated one of its Grand Dignatories of the 33° with the mission to prove if the Supreme Council of Egypt had been regularly constituted, and in the contrary case to proceed conformably to Article 5, sec. 3 of the General Statutes of 1786, which has been done.

That admitted, the Supreme Council of Italy is of opinion that Article 5 of the Treaty of Union of the Supreme Confederate Councils is entirely foreign to the Constitution of the Supreme Council of Egypt, which has had existence before the said Treaty.

The Supreme Council of Italy regrets exceedingly that political events should have prevented the meeting of the next Universal Masonic Congress, which ought to have taken place this year at London, for it would have given it all the information necessary to justify its actions in favor of the Supreme Council of Egypt. Nevertheless, it will not fail to give the information to the Supreme Confederate Councils, and will be very grateful to those who shall wish to accord it their approval.

You are not unaware, dear Sir and T∴ Ill∴ Bro∴, that our institution has enemies who make a mockery of truth and morality, leaving philanthropy entirely aside, and reducing Masonry to be henceforth only a political society which they use and abuse for their particular interest. It is, then, our duty to oppose them, and disentangle our respectable body from the elements which will end by dishonoring it.

To this end I confirm mine of 30th April last, No. 154.

Accept my fraternal salutations, &c., &c.

(Signed)   LA SALLE, 33°,
Grand Chancellor.

33, GOLDEN SQUARE, LONDON, W.
22nd May, 1878.

DEAR SIR AND ILL∴ BRO∴.

I have the honour to acknowledge the receipt of your favour of the 19th instant

This Supreme Council is unable to admit the right of the Supreme Council for Italy to recognize as a legitimate body any Supreme Council, not being a Member of the Confederation, without previously obtaining the assent of the whole of the Confederated Councils.

Had your proposition to recognize Egypt as a legitimate Body been duly circulated in conformity with the spirit of the Treaty of Alliance, this Supreme Council would have objected to the proposition, even if the Supreme Council of Egypt had originally been "legitimately created and established in conformity with the Grand Constitutions of 1786," owing to its having violated those Constitutions in granting a warrant for the establishment of a Supreme Council, 33°, in New Zealand, a Dependency of the British Crown; this act being a violation of territorial jurisdiction which every Member of the Confederation is, under Art. L, sec 4, of the Treaty of Alliance, bound to maintain and defend.

This Supreme Council feel compelled to decline to recognize the Supreme Council of Egypt as a regularly constituted Body, and consider it their bounden duty to protest against its recognition by your Supreme Council without the general consent of the Confederation.

I am directed to say, in conclusion, that this Supreme Council regard the circumstances of the present case to be so serious as to require them to circulate their remonstrance against your action to all Members of the Confederation.

I am, Sir,

(Signed)　　　HUGH D. SANDEMAN, 33°,

Gr∴ Sec∴ Foreign Correspondence.

To Ill∴ Bro∴ LA SALLE, Grand Chancellor
　　Sup∴ Coun∴ 33° for Italy.

True Copies.

HUGH D. SANDEMAN, 33°,

Gr∴ Sec∴ Foreign Correspondence.

Circular of the Supreme Council of the Southern Jurisdiction U. S. A., regarding the Supreme Council of Egypt :—

FIDUCIA NOSTRA EST IN DEO.

GRAND ORIENT OF WASHINGTON,

The 11th day of——A∴ M∴ 5638 ; 12th June, 1878, V∴ E∴

To the M∴ P∴ Sov∴ Grand Commander and Ill∴ Brethren of the Supreme Council of the 33d Degree for Canada.

The Supreme Council for the Southern Jurisdiction of the United States, at its meeting in May last, adopted the following resolution :

Resolved,—"That the Grand Orient of Egypt (as reorganized under proper " Masonic authority) be and is hereby acknowledged as a legitimate and lawful " authority. But this Supreme Council declines to enter into amicable relations " therewith until its position relative to the establishment of a Supreme Council " within the British possessions be more satisfactorily explained."

It is the settled opinion of our Supreme Council that either the Supreme Council of England and Wales and the Dependencies of the British Crown, alone, or that Supreme Council and those for Ireland and Scotland, have exclusive jurisdiction within the whole extent of all the Dependencies, Provinces and Colonies of Great Britain, everywhere in the world, except the Dominion of Canada ; and that no other Power of the Ancient and Accepted Scottish Rite can or ever could lawfully create a Supreme Council in any such Dependency, Province or Colony ; and that, therefore, the creation in New Zealand by the

Supreme Council of Egypt, of a body claiming to be a Supreme Council of the 33d degree, was a violation of the jurisdictional rights of the British Supreme Councils, unlawful and null ; and that the Body so established is irregular and illegal and has no lawful being as a Supreme Council.

The Supreme Council of Egypt is quite willing, we have reason to believe, to submit in this matter to the general judgment of the Supreme Powers of the Rite.   Unless and until their opinions are expressed, that Body ought, perhaps not to be expected to humiliate itself by admission of error and wrong, and by disowning its own progeny ; at least it will, we think, be better for the different Powers to give a definite and precise expression of opinion upon the question involved, and thus enable the Supreme Council of Egypt, if the general opinion should be against it, with alacrity and grace to submit to the judgment of its Peers.

The Supreme Council for the Southern Jurisdiction of the United States holds it to be, and submits to its sister Supreme Councils that it is, ·a settled principle of the law of the Ancient and Accepted Scottish Rite,

" That in a Dependency, Province or Colony of a Country in which there is a lawful Supreme Council, no foreign Power can create or authorize the creation of a Supreme Council ; and a Body so created as a Supreme Council has no legal existence"—

and hopes that it will please other Supreme Councils to express to that of Egypt their opinions upon this proposition.

May our Father which is in Heaven have you always in His holy keeping.

ALBERT PIKE, 33°,

Sov∴ Gr∴ Commander.

Decree of the Supreme Council of Egypt annulling its action in New Zealand, and in the matter of creating members of the 33° in Scotland, received since the session of this Sup∴ Council :—

GRAND ORIENT OF EGYPT.

Supreme Council of the 33d and last Degree of the A∴ & A∴ S∴ R∴

№. 152.   DÉCREE.

Valley of the Nile, Orient of Alexandria.

We, S. A. ZOLA, Sov∴ Gr∴ Com∴, Grand Master of the Supreme Council of the 33rd and last degree of the A∴ & A∴ S∴ R∴ for Egypt and its Dependencies.

Whereas the Supreme Council of Egypt, ever anxious to propagate the high principles of the Rite, by our decree No. 45, of the 16th Oct., 1875, and subsequently No. 69, of the 20th March, 1876, exalted to the 33° various distinct Masons, living in New Zealand, and granted their Patent by which they constituted themselves in that Valley as a Sup∴ Council of the 33°, and because we considered such territory as free and not subject to any regular Sup∴ Council ;

And whereas the Supreme Council of Egypt, by means of our various decrees, exalted to the 33° several Masons living in Scotland, because that Supreme Council was represented to us as an irregular and illegitimate Body ;

We being now persuaded and convinced of the legal and legitimate existence of the Supreme Councils of England, Ireland and Scotland and of the right of the first or of all the three over New Zealand, considered as a dependency of the British Crown, and consequently being anxious to repair the serious mistake into which we have inadvertently fallen ;

Having consulted the Grand Constitution of 1786—desirous that as far as in us lies the most perfect harmony should exist amongst all the Supreme Councils of both hemispheres—exacting for ourselves and for all Masonic Powers the most scrupulous reciprocity relating to the question of territorial jurisdiction ;

Desiring above all that not the least pretext of schism or division on our part should tend to rupture the universal Masonic alliance ;

We have decreed and do hereby decree :—

ARTICLE I.—Our decrees No. 45, of 16th October, 1875, and No. 69, of 20th March, 1876, by which we exalted to the 33° several Masons living in New Zealand and accorded them the facility of constituting themselves into a Supreme Council, 33°, are definitely abrogated.

ARTICLE II.—All our decrees by which were exalted by proxy, various Masons living in Scotland, have been annulled.

ARTICLE III.—All Patents, all Diplomas and all Certificates granted either for New Zealand or for Scotland by proxy and appertaining to the A∴ & A∴S∴ R∴ have been cancelled by the Mother Supreme Council, and are declared null.

ARTICLE IV.—These presents shall be communicated to the parties interested, and shall be despatched to all the Supreme Councils of both hemispheres, and published in our Official Bulletin.

Given at the Grand Orient of Cairo, Valley of the Nile, this 8th Tisri, A.M. 5638, commonly the 7th September, 1878.

(Signed)   A. S. ZOLA, 33°,
Sov∴ Gr∴ Com∴ Grand Master.

F. F. ADDIRZ, 33°,
Gr∴ Sec∴ General.

Supplemental Report of the Committee on Foreign Correspondence and Relations made since the session of this Supreme Council :—

Since the close of the Supreme Council information has been received that the Egyptian body, by formal decree, declares that it has " become aware of the grave error" into which it has fallen by the establishment of the New Zealand Council. It has " definitely annulled" the powers it gave " certain persons" to constitute themselves a Supreme Council for New Zealand. It has also annulled all decrees by which it has admitted (in absentia), to the highest degree of the Rite certain Masons in Scotland, and has recalled all patents, diplomas and certificates issued to these Masons. This unquestionably, paves the way for an early recognition of the Supreme Council for Egypt.

On behalf of Committee,

(Signed)   J. V. ELLIS, 33°,
Chairman.

TABLEAU

OF THE

SUPREME COUNCIL OF S.·. G.·. I.·. G.·. 33°,

FOR THE

→⁑DOMINION+OF+CANADA,⁑←

GRAND EAST, MONTREAL, PROVINCE OF QUEBEC.

1878-9.

OFFICERS.

T. DOUGLAS HARINGTON, 33°,

M.·. P.·. Sov. Gr.·. Commander.

ROBERT MARSHALL, 33°,

P.·. Lieut.·. Gr.·. Commander.

JOHN WALTER MURTON, 33°,

Ill.·. Secretary General H.·. E.·.

HUGH ALEXANDER MACKAY, 33°,

Ill.·. Treasurer General H.·. E.·.

JOHN VALENTINE ELLIS, 33°,

Ill.·. Grand Chancellor.

DAVID RANSOM MUNRO, 33°,

Ill.·. Grand Master of Ceremonies.

WILLIAM HENRY HUTTON, 33°,

Ill.·. Grand Marshal.

ISAAC HENRY STEARNS, 33°,

Ill.·. Grand Standard Bearer.

WILLIAM REID, 33°,

Ill.·. Grand Captain of the Guard.

DEPUTIES.

JOHN WALTER MURTON, 33°,
>   *Hamilton, for Province of Ontario.*

WILLIAM HENRY HUTTON, 33°,
>   *Montreal, for Province of Quebec.*

ROBERT MARSHALL, 33°,
>   *St. John, for Province of New Brunswick.*

BENJAMIN LESTER PETERS, 33°,
>   *St. John, for Province of Nova Scotia.*

ROBERT THOMSON CLINCH, 33°,
>   *St. John, for Province of Prince Edward Island.*

MEMBERS.

COL. W. J. B. MACLEOD MOORE, 33°,
>   *Laprairie, Province of Quebec.*

EUGENE M. COPELAND, 33°,
>   *Berthier En Haut, Province of Quebec.*

HUGH MURRAY, 33°,
>   *Hamilton, Province of Ontario.*

JAMES K. KERR, 33°,
>   *Toronto, Province of Ontario.*

JAMES DOMVILLE, 33°,
>   *St. John, Province of New Brunswick.*

HUGH WILLIAMS CHISHOLM, 33°,
>   *St. John, Province of New Brunswick.*

HONORARY MEMBERS.

DR. ROBERT HAMILTON, 33°,
>   *Supreme Council England, Wales, etc.*

HON. ALBERT PIKE, 33°,
>   *M∴ P∴ Sov∴ Gr∴ Com∴ Sup∴ Co∴ Southern Jurisdiction*
>   *U. S A.*

HON. JOSIAH H. DRUMMOND, 33°,
>   *M∴ P∴ Sov∴ Gr∴ Com∴ Sup∴ Co∴ Northern Jurisdiction U. S. A.*

JOHN FITZHENRY TOWNSHEND, 33°,
>   *M∴ P∴ Sov∴ Gr∴ Com∴ Sup∴ Co∴ Ireland.*

REPRESENTATIVES OF THIS SUPREME COUNCIL.

DR. ROBERT HAMILTON, 33°,
>   *London, England ; near the Supreme Council of England,*
>   *Wales, etc.*

DR. ALBERT G. MACKEY, 33°,
>   *Washington, D∴ C∴ near the Supreme Council of the*
>   *Southern Jurisdiction, U. S. A.*

D. BURHAM TRACY, 33°,
>   *Detroit, Michigan; near the Supreme Council of the Northern*
>   *Jurisdiction, U. S. A.*

LINDSAY MACKERSY, 33°,
>   *Edinburgh, Scotland; near the Supreme Council of Scotland.*

RIGHT HON. HEDGES EYRE CHATTERTON, 33°,
>   *Dublin, Ireland ; near the Supreme Council of Ireland.*

EMANUEL ARAGO, 33°,
>   *Paris, France; near the Supreme Council of France.*

EDOUARD CLUYDTS, 33°,
>   *Brussels, Belgium ; near the Supreme Council of Belgium.*

TIMOTHIE RIBOLI, 33°,
>   *Turin, Italy; near the Supreme Council of Italy.*

RICARDO H. HARTLEY, 33°,
>   . *Lima, Peru; near the Supreme Council of Peru.*

DR. ALEXANDER DAMASCHINO, 33°,
>   *Athens, Greece; near the Supreme Council of Greece.*

DR. LOUIS ALVAREZ, D'AZEVDO MACEDO, 33°,
>   *Rio de Janiero; near the Supreme Council of Brazil.*

FRANCOIS RAMUZ, 33°,
>   *Lausanne, Switzerland; near the Sup∴ Co∴ of Switzerland.*

F. W. RAMSDEN, 33°,
>   *S. Jago De Cuba; near the Supreme Council of Colon.*

REPRESENTATIVES OF FOREIGN SUPREME COUNCILS NEAR THIS SUPREME COUNCIL.

COL. W. J. B. MACLEOD MOORE, 33°,
>   *Laprairie, Quebec ; of the Sup∴ Councils of England, Wales,*
>   *Etc., and of Greece.*

JOHN WALTER MURTON, 33°,
  Hamilton, Ontario ; of the Supreme Councils of the Southern Jurisdiction, U. S. A., and of Belgium.

HUGH ALEXANDER MACKAY, 33°,
  Hamilton, Ontario ; of the Supreme Council of the Northern Jurisdiction, U. S. A.

ROBERT MARSHALL, 33°,
  St. John, New Brunswick ; of the Sup.·. Co.·. of Peru.

JOHN VALENTINE ELLIS, 33°,
  St. John, New Brunswick ; of the Sup.·. Co.·. of Scotland.

JAMES DOMVILLE, 33°,
  St. John, New Brunswick ; of the Sup.·. Council of Ireland.

GRAND BODIES IN CORRESPONDENCE WITH THIS SUPREME COUNCIL.

Supreme Council of England, Wales, Etc.
Supreme Council of Southern Jurisdiction, U. S. A.
Supreme Council of Northern Jurisdiction, U. S. A.
Supreme Council of Scotland.
Supreme Council of Ireland.
Supreme Council of France.
Supreme Council of Belgium.
Supreme Council of Italy.
Supreme Council of Peru.
Supreme Council of Colon for the West India Islands.
Supreme Council of Brazil.
Supreme Council of Switzerland.
Supreme Council of Greece.
Supreme Council of New Grenada.
Supreme Council of Mexico.

SUBORDINATE BODIES

UNDER THE

⁕JURISDICTION ✛ OF ✛ THIS ✛ SUPREME ✛ COUNCIL⁕

→1878.←

ONTARIO.

MOORE CONSISTORY, 32°, Hamilton.

J. W. Murton, 33°, Com-in-Chief.   J. II. Tilden, 32°, Gr∴ Sec∴

HAMILTON CHAPTER ROSE CROIX, 18°, Hamilton.

John M. Gibson, 32°, M∴ W∴ Sov.   William Bowman, 31°, Registrar.

MURTON LODGE OF PERFECTION, 14°, Hamilton.

Gavin Stewart, 32°, T∴ P∴ Gr∴ M∴   Allan Land, 18°, Secretary.

LONDON CHAPTER ROSE CROIX, 18°, London.

George S. Birrell, 32°, M∴ W∴ Sov∴   H. A. Baxter, 31°, Registrar.

TORONTO CHAPTER ROSE CROIX, 18°, Toronto.

Richard J. Hovenden, 32°, M∴ W∴ Sov∴   Ulysses Boddy, 18°, Registrar.

TORONTO LODGE OF PERFECTION, 14°, Toronto.

Thos. F. Blackwood, 31°, T∴ P∴ Gr∴ M∴   T. D. Ledyard, 18°, Gr∴ Sec∴

QUEBEC.

MONTREAL CONSISTORY, 32°, Montreal.

Wm. H. Hutton, 33°, Com-in-Chief.   G. H. Wainwright, 32°, Gr∴ Sec∴

Hochelaga Chapter Rose Croix, 18°, Montreal.

Wm. H. Hutton, 33°, M.·. W.·. Sov.·.   W. Simpson Walker, 32°,'Registrar.

Hochelaga Lodge of Perfection, 14°, Montreal.

Charles Geo. Geddes, 32°, T.·.P.·.Gr.·.M.·.   W. Simpson Walker, 32°, Gr.·.Sec.·.

NEW BRUNSWICK.

New Brunswick Consistory, 32°, St. John.

David R. Munro, 33°, Com-in-Chief.   Wm. J.. Logan, 32°, Gr.·. Secretary.

Harington Chapter Rose Croix, 18°, St. John.

B. Lester Peters, 33°, M.·. W.·. Sov.·.   T. Nisbet Robertson, 30°, Registrar.

St. John Lodge of Perfection, 14°, St. John.

John V. Ellis, 33°, T.·. P.·. Gr.·. M.·.   Secretary.

NOVA SCOTIA.

Keith Chapter Rose Croix, 18°, Halifax.

os. Norman Ritchie, 18°, M.·. W.·. Sov.·.   Geo. T. Smithers, 18°, Registrar.

MEMBERS

ON THE

❖ᐻREGISTER❖OF❖THIS❖SUPREME❖COUNCIL,❖ᐻ

31st AUGUST, 1878.

Ardell, James - - - -	18°	Baker, Charles P. - -	30°
Adam, James - - -	18°	Brown, Silas Harrington - -	30°
Adams, James - - -	14°	Boyd, Herbert, M.D. - -	32°
Andrews, John Wm. - -	18°	Brown, Charles W. - -	18°
Almon, Rev. H. P. - -	18°	Bryan, Wm. J. - - -	18°
Albertson, Ransom B. -	18°	Boddy, Ulysses - - -	18°
Alexander, Thos. K. - -	32°	Bentley, Lewis - - -	14°
Adcock, Thomas - -	30°	Bond, Frank - - -	32°
Angus, Richard B. - -	32°	Brown, John - - -	14°
Alexander, Henry M. - -	31°	Bell, David - - - -	14°
Aitchison, David - -	14°	Brent, Geo. Walter - -	14°
Adams, James - - -	18°	Beckett, Henry M. - - -	4°
Birge, Charles A. - - -	32°	Charlton, James - - -	32°
Brierly, Richard - -	32°	Carey, William - - -	32°
Bartindale, Thos. H. - -	18°	Caulfield, Rev. St. George -	30°
Biggar, Wm. F. - -	18°	Caw, William - - -	18°
Bowman, Wm. - -	31°	Chisholm, Hugh W. - -	33°
Babcock, Brenton D. - -	33°	Clinch, Robert T. - -	33°
Bruce, Wm. - - -	18°	Carritto, Thomas W., M.D. -	18°
Boultbee, John - - -	18°	Chamberlain, Montague -	31°
Beasley, Thomas - -	18°	Clarke, Peter Parlee - -	18°
Bull, Richard - - -	32°	Clark, James Alfred - -	18°
Birrell, Geo. S. - -	32°	Crookshank, Robt. W. - -	32°
Beattie, Thomas - -	32°	Chesley, John Alex. - -	18°
Butterworth, Enoch B. -	32°	Crossman, Theodore A. -	18°
Brydon, Wm. - - -	32°	Cameron, Wm. James - -	18°
Blackwood, Thos. F. - -	31°	Cooper, W. M. - - -	14°
Baxter, Hamilton A. - -	31°	Copeland, Eugene M. -	33°
Burch, David B. - -	31°	Clouston, Edward T. - -	32°
Byron, Benjamin - - -	18°	Claggett, Charles C. - -	32°
Bartlett, Rev. Henry -	18°	Cushing, Francis - -	32°
Burnett, John - - -	18°	Campbell, Alexander - -	14°
Bray, William T. - -	4°	Canfield, James - - -	14°
Bull, William - - -	4°	Cameron, James C. - -	14°
Bosant, Christopher - -	18°		
Barteaux, E. Lawrence, M.D.	18°	Duncan, Alexander - -	32°
Beatty, John Howard - -	18°	Despard, Fitzherbert R -	32°

Dewar, William	32°
Davidson, Charles	16°
Dalley, Fenner Frederick	18°
Davis, Evans	18°
Domville, James	33°
DeVeber, J. S. Boies	18°
Dolphin, Kellam James	12°
Darby, George	18°
Dixon, Wm. J.	14°
Davies, John Try	32°
Dewar, David B.	14°
Davis, Cornelius A.	14°
Edgar, Wm.	32°
Eckerson, Luther	18°
Englehart, Jacob L.	18°
Ellis, John Valentine	33°
Earle, Sylvester Z., M. D.	18°
Everett, Edwin J.	32°
Ellis, James F.	31°
Erskine, John	18°
Edwards, George O.	32°
Edgar, Frank	32°
Furness, Peter S.	18°
Foster, Charles H.	18°
Fisher, John	30°
Fleming, William	18°
Forster, Thos. A. D.	18°
Foster, Wm. D.	32°
Fraser, George	18°
Fishwick, Fredk. Wm.	18°
Fleming, William	30°
Fulford, Henry	18°
Falkiner, Nathl. B.	4°
Fergusson, John S.	4°
Gibson, John M.	32°
Gibson, Robert Lillis	18°
Goodhue, Charles F.	30°
Goodwin, Alfred D.	32°
Godsoe, Thos. Amos	30°
Godsoe, William C.	30°
Gorham, Edward	18°
Gossip, James	18°
Graham, John H.	32°
Guy, John G. W.	31°
Girdwood, Gilbert P., M.D.	32°
Geddes, Charles G.	32°
Gray, John	32°
Gracie, John	14°
Humphrey, Nelson	18°
Hutchison, Robert A.	32°
Halson, Robert	18°
Hope, Robert Knight	32°
Harington, Thos. Douglas	33°
Hyndman, William	18°
Hewson, George H.	30°
Hills, Rolland	18°
Hutton, William Henry	33°
Hovenden, Richard J.	32°
Heron, James	18°
Hood, Frederick J.	18°
Hunt, Charles B.	18°
Hyman, Charles S.	18°
Hatheway, Joseph C.	32°
Hesson, Wm. Alex.	18°
Hart, Wm. Henry	18°
Hesslein, Alex. George	18°
Harman, Saml. B.	18°
Howel, Augustus T.	18°
Hamilton, Wm. Jr.	18°
Hambly, Wm. Jas.	18°
Hutchinson, Thomas	18°
Henderson, James D.	18°
Hagar, Charles W.	32°
Henshaw, Fredk. C.	32°
Holton, Edward	18°
Hyndman, Hugh	14°
Irving, Andrew S.	30°
Irwin, John	18°
Isaacson, John H.	32°
Jamieson, W. R.	4°
Jones, Wm. John M.	30°
Johnson, Samuel	18°
Kerns, Wm.	18°
Kerr, James K.	33°
Kilvert, Francis E.	30°
Kennedy, Reginald	18°
Kerr, Wm.	32°
Kingsmill, Geo. R.	18°
Kerr, Murray A.	14°
Land, John Henry	18°
Leith, Wm.	18°
Land, Allan	18°
Lewis, Robert	18°
Lawrence, Bela R.	32°
Leonard, J. Henry	32°
Logan, Wm. J.	32°
Ledyard, Thomas D.	18°
Leask, John	14°
Liddell, Geo. W.	30°
Lazier, Stephen F.	16°
Lyon, Napoleon, T.	4°
London, Wm. H. S.	4°
Murton, John W.	33°
Mackay, Hugh A.	33°
Murray, Hugh	33°
Moore, Col. W. J. B. Macleod	33°
Marshall, Robert	33°

Munro, David R.	- - -	33°
Munday, Wm. T.	- - -	32°
Mitchell, Edward	-	31°
Murray, Charles R.	-	32°
Menet, Fred. Jas.	- - -	32°
Mason, John J.	- - -	32°
Morris, Wm. J.	- - -	18°
Mason, Joseph	- - -	31°
Meakins, Jonathan M.	-	31°
Macallum, Archd. M.	-	31°
Matheson, Walter	-	18°
Morgan, Benj. J.	- - -	18°
Milward, Wm. E., M.D.	-	18°
Moffat, James	- - -	32°
Macbeth, John	- - -	30°
Mackenzie, Capt Colin	-	18°
Mullin John	- - -	18°
Melick, John	- - -	18°
Murray, Christopher	-	30°
Munro, William	-	18°
Mathews, Saml. F.	-	18°
Macaw, John	- - -	18°
Murray, Wm. Erskine	-	13°
Morden, Albert Milton	-	14°
Macklin, Marshall M.D.	-	14°
Matheson, J. D.	-	14°
Morgan, J. V.	- - -	30°
Molson, John W.	- - -	32°
Mussen, Henry S.	-	18°
Munro, Colin	- - -	14°
McLellan, David	-	32°
McLelland, Wm.	- -	18°
McPhie, Donald	- -	31°
McClure, James F.	-	18°
McKay, Robert	- -	18°
McNichol, James J.	-	18°
McLeod, William	-	18°
McClelland, Thos. J.	-	16°
McCord, David R.	-	32°
McKenzie, Daniel	-	9°
McLaren, Alexander	-	9°
McKeand, Alfred	-	14°
McCrae, Colin	- -	14°
McLean, Donald	- -	4°
Northey, Geo. V.	-	18°
Niven, James S., M.D.	-	18°
Neely, James	- -	18°
Nivin, William	- -	32°
Nelson, Albert D.	-	32°
Nixon, James B.	-	30°
Neave, Spencer Le Neave	-	18°
Orpen, Henry John	-	16°
O'Halleran, James	-	18°
Patterson, George H.	-	18°

Priddis, James	- - -	30°
Porte, Andrew W.	- - -	18°
Peters, Benj. Lester	-	33°
Potter, Charles E.	-	18°
Partridge, Rev. Francis		32°
Porteaus, Charles E. L.	-	18°
Purvis, Joseph	-	18°
Patterson, Geo. Carson	-	18°
Perkins, Arthur M.	-	18°
Pain, Albert	- -	14°
Reid, Wm.	- - -	33°
Robertson, James	-	31°
Robb, Thomas B.	-	18°
Richardson, Charles	-	16°
Robinson, T. Barclay	-	18°
Robertson, James Hay	-	18°
Rankin, Alexander	-	30°
Ring, Geo. Frederick	-	18°
Reed, Thomas M.	-	30°
Robertson, Thomas Nisbet	-	30°
Ritchie, Jos. Norman	-	18°
Richards, Wm. Walton	-	18°
Robb, Rev. J. G.	-	18°
Reed, Joseph B.	-	18°
Robertson, John A.	-	32°
Reynolds, Thomas J.	-	18°
Russell, George	-	14°
Stewart, Gavin	-	32°
Smith, Charles R.		32°
Smith, Alfred W.	-	18°
Spencer, Walter	-	31°
Scott, John	-	18°
Stuart, Wm. R.	-	18°
Stephenson, James	-	32°
Spry, Daniel	-	32°
Smyth, Alfred G.	-	30°
Sargant, Thomas	-	32°
Smylie, Robert W.	-	31°
Smith, Wm. Simpson	-	18°
Shurman, John D.	-	18°
Shantz, Abraham B.	-	4°
Smith David G.	-	32°
Scovil, James	-	30°
Stewart, George J.	-	18°
Scovil Rev. Wm.	-	32°
Stewart David Smith	-	32°
Sircom, Stephen R.	-	32°
Smithers, George Thos.	-	18°
Scholfield, John	-	18°
Sterling, Roland M.	-	18°
Simpson, William	-	17°
Stephens, Richard P.	-	16°
Stevenson, Jas. D., M.D.	-	18°
Slack, Jos. A.	-	18°
Stearns, Isaac H.	-	33°
Sinclair, David	-	32°

Simpson, Wm. B. - - 32°	Whyte, Alex. Ralph - - 32°
Sutherland, Louis - - - 32°	Wright, Hugh McC. - ▪ 31°
Smith, David A. ▪ - - 18°	Widger, James - - - 18°
Stewart. Adam A. - - - 14°	Wilson, Archdale - - 18°
Sheriff, Andrew - - - 4°	Wright, Edward H. ▪ - 18°
	Willson, Arthur L. - - 30°
Tilden, John H - - - 32°	Waterman, Herman - - 18°
Thompson, John H. - - 32°	Willis, Edward - - - 30°
Tracy, Thos. H. - - - 18°	Wetmore, Edwin J. ▪ - 30°
Taylor, John - - - 14°	Wilson, J. Newton - - ▪ 18°
Thorne, Wm. Henry - ▪ 32°	Wisdom, Freeman W. - - 30°
Thornton, John N, - - 18°	Watson, George - - - 18°
Taylor, John Miles - - - 18°	Wilson, James - - - 18°
Tennant, David ▪ - - 18°	Watson, William - - - 18°
Trayes, John B. - - - 14°	Winans, Edward C. - - 4°
	Wallace, Wm. B. - ▪ - 14°
Vail, Albert S, - - - 18°	Whitehead, Edward A. ▪ 32°
Vroom, William E. - ▪ 18°	Wainwright, Geo. H. R. - 32°
Vose, Charles F. - - - 18°	Walker, Wm. Simpson ▪ 32°
Venables, John H. - - 18°	Warner, John F. · - - 18°
	Willson, Isaac P. - - 14°
Wright, John - ▪ - - 18°	